My Four Worlds

My Four Worlds

SMART EZE

authorHOUSE®

AuthorHouse™ UK Ltd.
500 Avebury Boulevard
Central Milton Keynes, MK9 2BE
www.authorhouse.co.uk
Phone: 08001974150

First published by AuthorHouse 2/18/2011

ISBN: 978-1-4520-5077-5 (sc)
ISBN: 978-1-4520-9813-5 (e)

This book is printed on acid-free paper.

To My Reader

I realize that everyone definitely has a story to tell about themselves. But I was encouraged to write my story by people who have heard me tell it on many occasions and at different forums.

I have told my story to young people at workshops in schools, to adult men and women in public platforms, on radio and television programmes, and in newspapers. They have found my story interesting and worthy of being told again and again. I agree with them that my story is a genuine example of how to face the challenges of life during our journey from cradle to grave.

Despite the woes, gnashing of teeth, despairs, and disappointments we may encounter on our journey, we should not at any time give up our hope of success, but be resolute in our struggle because we shall emerge triumphant and jubilant at the end with the vindication that every disappointment may be a blessing.

I have recounted my story in four episodes. I begin with my services to the United Nations. I follow with my enthusiasm to catch up with my ambitions, and continue with the period of deprivation and devastation of my ego. I finish up with the romances of my childhood. I have written the highlights of my journey at the beginning and the end of each episode, so each one transitions into the next one. I invite you to join me in this exciting journey of life in my four worlds.

The Meritorious Services

It was an ordinary winter morning in February. The weather was bitterly cold, and there had been a heavy snowfall. I walked into my office and quickly dropped my briefcase on the desk so that I could tackle a routine and an important priority of the day for me in such a weather condition—I took my guide dog Nello straightaway to the washing room and washed his legs to remove the salts from his paws and protect him from unnecessary wounds and injury.

We returned to my office, and Nello went straight to his special bed under the table for a morning rest after the long winter journey from our home. I opened the cabinet and hung up my jacket and winter coat and changed shoes. It was time to sit at the desk, to open the drawers, and to switch on the electronics—a personal computer, a printer, and various adaptive technology devices for the blind.

As the equipment was starting up, the telephone rang. From its short interval peeps, I recognized that it was an internal call. I picked up the receiver, wondering who my first caller of the day might be. A female voice said, 'Good morning, Mr. Eze. This is the office of the director-general. The director-general would like you to come to his meeting room at eleven o'clock today. Will you be available?' I said, 'Yes, definitely', because I thought this time I knew fairly well the reason for such an emergency meeting with the head of our organization in Vienna.

Some ten minutes before eleven o'clock, I brought out my jacket from the cabinet and put it on, called up Nello from his place, and dressed him up in his harness, which was his working gear. Quickly, we walked over to the director-general's office in time for the appointment. As I came into the room, I sensed that a number of familiar colleagues were already seated at the table, including the head of my department, the chiefs of administration, security services, protocol, the spokesman, and the photographer. I was ushered to a chair, where I sat down and asked Nello to lie down quietly next to me. Everyone chatted and waited for the director-general to arrive.

The room was solemnly quiet as the director-general entered and walked straight across and sat in his chair. I sensed that all eyes were focused on me as he began to speak. 'Mr. Eze, we have gathered here to say goodbye and to thank you for your contributions to the work of the United Nations.' He continued, 'The secretary-general has directed me to present you with this certificate of dedicated services to the United Nations. This is a unique occasion as it is in recognition of your almost twenty-five years of meritorious services to the organization, despite your physical disability.'

The director-general walked over to me and handed me the certificate and other memorabilia on behalf of the United Nations office at Vienna where I had begun my professional career in 1980. I was now to retire in 2005. Everyone around the table came over and congratulated me. There were pre-lunch refreshments and toasting, as well as group photo opportunity.

The week continued to be marked with a series of special events to bid me farewell. My department, the External Relations Section, organized a luncheon to which colleagues from other sections of our organization, the UN Office on Drugs and Crime, were invited. I was given memorabilia that included a booklet in which each colleague said nice words and expressed best wishes for me for the future.

The climax of the celebrations was a gala evening organized on my behalf by friends from all the organizations based at the Vienna International Centre. Friends and colleagues in the building and guests from the city of Vienna assembled to bid me farewell and present me with a number of souvenirs and a booklet of well wishes.

I reflected on the week's events and felt satisfied with the ways things had turned out for me. My almost twenty-five years of services to the UN had come and passed by quickly. *Retired but not tired*, I contemplated. For me, retirement had a special meaning. It meant the fulfilment of a long phase in my life and the beginning of a new and equally promising one.

When I finished my university studies and set off in search for a job, I could not imagine that my first employment would be with the UN; never mind that I would maintain that position until I was sixty years old. The circumstances were ripe: I was at the right place at the right time to secure the job. Before that, I was on the verge of giving up the job adventure out of frustration. The job market seemed to be completely closed to me as a totally blind person. At worst, my academic qualification seemed to be an obstacle rather than a facilitator in my quest, as I could not find a position commensurate with my abilities.

The excuses given by some of the employers were bizarre

and naive: We have no usable equipment for the blind. How can you plug in the electric cable without causing short circuit and fire hazard to yourself and others? We have no one to take you to and from the toilet and the restaurant every day. You can't travel unaided from and to the office. The list continued with seemingly insurmountable problems posed by the pessimists. I understood that, to succeed, I must meet these and other challenges resolutely.

I certainly cherished the actions of various individuals in helping me meet the challenges of seeing with the mind's eye. At the suggestion of an acquaintance, I boldly picked up the phone one morning in February 1980 and telephoned the home of the Austrian Federal Chancellor Bruno Kreisky. To my astonishment, he answered the telephone himself even though he was having breakfast, as it was still half past eight o'clock. I quickly introduced myself, not being quite sure what his reaction might be. He remembered me as the totally blind African who, only a few months ago in December 1979, had graduated from the Vienna University with a doctorate degree in philosophy. The event had been widely reported in the local and national news media.

I briefly explained to the federal chancellor my frustration over the difficulties in getting a job since my graduation. He listened patiently and asked me to call his spokesman and arrange a date to come and see him in his office. I took a mental note of the telephone numbers that he dictated to me. Before hanging up, I apologized to the federal chancellor for disturbing him so early in the morning and interrupting his breakfast. He said it was all in order and urged me not to worry—that he looked forward to meeting me personally and discussing my problems in his office. Actually, when I first learned, through my acquaintance, about the federal chancellor's openness to his fellow citizens, I did not imagine that he would equally extend this courtesy to me, since I was a foreigner and practically had no influence over his political career.

On the morning of the arranged day at ten o'clock, I arrived by taxi at the gate of Ballhausplatz, the location of the federal chancellor's office. I stepped out of the taxi, and the security guard escorted me to the receptionist's desk, where the spokesman was already waiting for me. We greeted each other and walked together through the hallway to the main office and to the meeting room of the chancellor.

The door to the meeting room opened and we walked in. It was quiet and empty. I could feel that it had been set up for an occasion. The air was filled with a strong smell of aromatic Viennese coffee and delicious pastries. The spokesman assisted me to a comfortably cushioned seat, and I sat down. The secretary walked in and treated me to a cup of coffee and some pastries, saying that the chancellor would be with us shortly.

I was just finishing my coffee and pastry when the federal chancellor came into the room and walked straight to me. I quickly wanted to stand up, but he politely asked me to remain seated in my chair. Finally I could not resist getting up when I noticed that he was already there standing in front of me. He shook my hand and walked to a chair to sit down. The atmosphere in the room was calm and friendly. But I was full of anxiety, though composed and trying very hard to fix my mind so I would be able to speak in a very clear and understandable language.

The federal chancellor requested that his secretary join the meeting and take down the minutes of the discussion. He recalled our earlier telephone discussion and asked me to describe my problems in greater detail. I complied and narrated to him the full story of my life both in Africa and Europe.

The UN had moved a number of programmes to its

newly established third headquarters in Vienna. One of these entities was the Centre for Social Development and Humanitarian Affairs. Its Disabled Persons Unit was responsible for organizing activities for the observance of the 1981 International Year of Disabled Persons.

The federal chancellor contemplated a while and suddenly burst forth with two brilliant ideas: Firstly, I was well placed to contribute to UN efforts for the observance of the International Year of Disabled Persons (IYDP). His argument was based on the fact that I originated from a developing country and was a disabled person myself and could be an asset and a good motivator for governments and communities in both developed and developing countries. Secondly, I could remain in the academic field with the University of Vienna, where I excelled in linguistic research. He encouraged me to apply for appropriate employment openings at these places and promised to support my endeavours.

Before I began my job search, I decided that a guide dog would enhance my mobility and help me to meet several of the formidable challenges of the pessimists in my quest for a job. I went to a guide dog school in Germany, which was recommended to me by a blind acquaintance. I was introduced to Ingo, my prospective guide dog. He was a twenty-month-old German shepherd dog, impressive, stoutly built, and self-confident—a no nonsense canine.

Ingo and I quickly tuned to each other and became friends. I was very surprised at this behaviour, as I had no prior experience with canine culture. But I quickly sensed that my professional career was going to be shaped in partnership with this dedicated canine friend. I trained with Ingo for two weeks at the school. The curriculum included learning thirty basic commands and skills for navigation, clearance of obstacles, indoor and outdoor disciplinary measures, physical fitness for dog walks, and general canine health and grooming procedures.

I returned to Vienna with the trainer for a further one-week training in my dwelling place. Ingo was introduced to my entire household. My wife Renate, a passionate animal lover and a schoolteacher, and Esther, my five-year-old daughter, welcomed him as a new member of our family.

He was taken around the flat and to his designated place with a comfortable mattress dressed up in a colourful bed sheet. He quickly lay down and seemed to love it.

The training in the city of Vienna was rigorous and intensive. The people and vehicle traffic in the peak time was very challenging. But Ingo was a star in full control of his profession. With ease and confidence, he accomplished the tasks of locating lifts and staircases, door handles, tram and bus stops; identifying zebra crossings; and manipulating multiple road junctions.

As a team, our performance on the roads, on trams, and in the parks was so unique that people stared at us and made friendly gestures. At this juncture, the trainer was prompted to comment that even the federal president would not be able to attract attention in the public at that level. When our training was complete, I felt more confident and secure than ever before as I moved around the city.

The next challenge expressed by the pessimistic job interviewers was seemingly more difficult to confront. But an innovative access technology product for blind people had just been released onto the market: Optacon was a portable electronic device that permitted blind people to read printed material. It consisted of a main electronics unit connected by a thin cable to a lens module. I was trained to use the device, which proved more demanding than the training with Ingo.

The main electronics unit contained a tactile array platform, on which I placed my index finger. When I moved the lens module across a printed line, the image underneath was transmitted through the connecting cable to the main electronics unit. I 'felt' the image of a printed letter moving under my index finger across the tactile array from right to left. The tactile array contained a matrix of tiny metal rods, which vibrated to form a magnified tactile representation of the image viewed by the lens. Even though I could not master reading a printed page in less than fifteen minutes, the reading skill I acquired was sufficient to convince the pessimists beyond reasonable doubts.

On one Friday afternoon in the summer of 1980, I returned from a visit with my family to my parents-in-law's home when the telephone rang. I picked up the receiver and a male voice said, 'This is the UN in Vienna. Can I speak to Mr. Smart Eze?' I replied, 'Yes, I am the one speaking.' I could tell he was smiling as he quietly said, 'You applied for the position of social affairs officer with the Centre for Social Development and Humanitarian Affairs some months ago. Are you still available?' Amused, I answered, 'Yes, definitely.' He asked me to come to the headquarters of the UN at Vienna the following Monday at nine o'clock in the morning and gave me the exact directions on how to get to the personnel department.

I arrived at the security gate of the Vienna International Centre where a staff member of the personnel department met me. Together we walked to the office of the chief of recruitment in the personnel department. My meeting with him was brief and courteous. I was then escorted to the upper floor of the building housing the Centre for Social Development and Humanitarian Affairs where I was introduced to the secretary of the International Year of Disabled Persons in her office. She offered me a chair, and I sat down. Ingo settled comfortably beside me. I was prepared for this job interview considering my previous negative experience with potential employers.

In her introductory remark, she explained to me, 'We are a small unit within the Centre for Social Development and Humanitarian Affairs. And we are responsible for organizing the International Year of Disabled Persons.' She continued, 'As a focal point on disability matters within the UN system, we advise countries and organizations on activities to be undertaken to make the International Year a success. Our work involves a lot of reading and writing, as well as travelling,' she concluded.

I was surprised when she invited me to say what the unit could do to help me in carrying out my part of the tasks. I expressed my appreciation for the opportunity given to me and explained to her what my priority needs were in that regard. Finally, she said that the personnel department would communicate with me as soon as her unit could have my priority working needs organized.

In early September, I received a letter of appointment with the UN. I was politely requested to report for official duty on 13 October 1980 at the UN in Vienna. I was filled with joy and excitement. It was going to be my first real working experience in life. So I made sure that I prepared myself solidly to meet the challenge, both physically and psychologically. I rehearsed all the training modules for the teamwork with Ingo, and reflected on the working environment of the UN and how I would fit in as a disabled person.

My first day in the office was filled with procedural matters. The administrative assistant was at hand to usher me into my office room. She provided me UN standard office equipment and accessories, such as a typewriter and a standard tape recorder, and showed me the location of the individual items in the room.

My initial working tools were an Optacon, a Perkins Brailler, a tape recorder adapted for the blind, and a portable pocket dictating and recording machine, which I brought with me from my home as they could not be provided to me by the organization at that time. Ingo's bed was settled under the table, the mattress decorated with a beautiful cover sheet. Barely settled down, I was called up to the personnel department to sign an agreement for a three-month contract with the UN.

Writing and reading documents were the greatest challenge in my daily work. Mobility was not too much of a problem since Ingo was always available to guide me anywhere in the building. I knew I must be creative, and improvisation became the order of the day. So I devised a variety of methods in preparing written documents: the texts were first prepared in Braille using the Perkins Brailler and then read out orally to the secretary to write down; I pre-recorded the texts on the recording machine and passed the cassettes on to the secretary so she could type out the contents; I used the secretary as amanuensis for direct and quick oral dictation. For longer documents, I typed the texts directly onto my typewriter; the disadvantage was that I could neither review nor edit the texts myself since they were in normal print. In meetings and similar activities outside my office, I frequently used the pocket recording and dictating machine for note taking.

There was a great amount of reading involved in this position. Large and numerous documents and general information material were routed to me daily. They originated from non-governmental organizations and the general public, various governments, the UN system, and particularly the Secretariat. I was required to read every piece of material so I could determine its importance and purpose, either for action or simply for information and education. A great number of them were in volumes of pages that took considerable hours to read. My reading speed with the Optacon was too slow for it to be a meaningful help. It was stressful to use and it wasted a great deal of my valuable working time, which I could hardly afford as one of the key professional staff members of the department.

Eventually, I put an announcement on the staff bulletin board for volunteer readers. The response was overwhelming. I had a sufficient number of volunteers from the different organizations in the building, as well as from private individuals outside the building, coming to read materials to me in my office during lunch breaks and after official working hours. Some readers took the materials home and recorded them for me. The secretary read the internal documents to me, such as letters for correction, memoranda, and confidential correspondence for information. So I established a viable system for mastering the huge number of UN documents that streamed daily into my office demanding immediate action on my part.

Now Ingo's requirements had to be taken care of as well, and his working environment adjusted appropriately. It was not easy for him to be the only canine staff member in the midst of over 5,000 human colleagues plus another more than 2,000 visitors in the building daily. Our first hurdle was in the cafeteria, which was always packed full with people at lunchtime. These were staff members, people attending various conferences in the building, as well as visitors. They walked frantically in all directions carrying their trays of food and looking for their companions and free tables. Ingo would guide me through them all with unimaginable precision in search of a free table. Once he found one, he would charge forward dragging me along tenderly to occupy it.

Naturally, some of the people were not accustomed to dogs, and others did not expect to meet a dog in such a place. In both instances, some were scared if Ingo arrived to share a table with them for lunch. As his head was habitually higher than the dining tables, the smell of the delicious foods on the trays unresistingly invited his nuzzling nose. The courageous ones stayed in their chairs, but the respectful ones jumped from their chairs, lifting their food trays to look for another free place.

To remedy such a scenario and to help Ingo avoid having to go to different tables in search of a free chair each time we arrived for lunch, a table was especially set up in the cafeteria with a bold sign reading Reserved for Mr. Eze and His Guide Dog, Ingo.

Our second hurdle was how Ingo would be identified coming in and going out of the building if I did not accompany him. With due regard to the canine culture, he must be given enough opportunity to exercise and to perform his regular necessities. I walked him on the grass in front of the building in the mornings and evenings, and in the Donau Park for longer walks at lunchtime. If I sat in a meeting that extended over the lunch period, I would ask someone to kindly take Ingo out for a walk. On several occasions, Ingo was refused entry into the building by the security guard at the gate because animals were not permitted on the premises according to buildings administrative rules. Each time I was called upon to identify my guide dog since he was not dressed up in his working gear. So a practical solution was devised to the satisfaction of all concerned. Ingo, just like every other staff member, was issued a Vienna International Centre (VIC) Grounds Pass bearing his picture, name, and relevant details.

It was time to formally welcome Ingo and me to the UN environment at the Vienna International Centre since we had now settled down comfortably in our office. Our appearance on the stage seemed to have provided a noticeable booster to the objectives of the 1981 International Year of Disabled Persons as was rightly predicted by the Austrian federal chancellor when I visited him in his office.

The United Nations Industrial Development Organisation (UNIDO) staff journal, the UN staff forum, and *Echo*, the International Atomic Energy Agency (IAEA) staff journal all carried headline news articles about my guide dog and me, acknowledging Ingo as the 'first four-legged UN staff member'. The story was immediately picked up by the international news media. Articles and pictures about my guide dog and me in action were extensively covered in local magazines and newspapers around the globe. Before I knew it, the pressure was mounting, and my mission had begun. I was expected to be a true ambassador for how to overcome the limitations of disability in all its facets.

My job focused principally on external relations and public information. These were two identical fields of responsibility through which I should substantially contribute in my own way to improving the image of disabled persons worldwide. An important message of the year was that the image of disabled persons depended to a great extent on the fact that social attitudes were a major barrier to the realization of their goal of full participation and equality in society. But, before I could take a full plunge into the job, I had to acquaint myself with the history of the UN programme on disability.

In the aftermath of the Second World War, the UN Secretariat and the Economic and Social Council were the principal UN bodies concerned with disability issues. In its initial work on disability, the UN promoted a welfare perspective of disability. It established mechanisms for developing suitable programmes to deal with disability issues. But, as a result of policy re-evaluation, the focus was quickly shifted from a welfare perspective to one of social welfare.

Although these early activities supported the right of disabled persons to welfare and public services, little attention was given to obstacles that might be created by those goals in society. With the adoption of the Declaration on Social Progress and Development in 1969, attitudes began to shift towards a new social model for dealing with disability.

The concept of human rights for disabled persons began to be accepted internationally. This trend was affirmed in two major declarations adopted by the UN General Assembly: the Declaration on the Rights of Mentally Retarded Persons (1971) and the Declaration on the Rights of Disabled Persons (1975).

In 1976, the UN General Assembly proclaimed 1981 as the International Year of Disabled Persons (IYDP). It called for a plan of action at the national, regional, and international levels, with an emphasis on equalization of opportunities, rehabilitation, and prevention of disabilities.

The theme of the Year was "'Full Participation and Equality', defined as the right of disabled persons to take part fully in the life and development of their societies, to enjoy living conditions equal to those of other citizens, and to have an equal share in improved conditions resulting from social and economic development.

Further objectives of the Year were to increase public awareness, to understand and accept disabled persons, and to encourage disabled persons to form organizations through which they could express their views and promote action to improve their situation.

Such was the setting in which I had to carry out my duties; as a blind person, I was all the more conscious of the objectives of the Year. I wrote letters and cables to governments, individuals, and organizations, I researched and prepared reports for intergovernmental bodies, and I prepared interoffice memoranda at various levels.

Organizations, especially those of disabled persons in developing countries, needed technical and financial support as well as encouragement in their actions. Governments, in their respective countries, were given guidance in the interpretation and implementation of the activities recommended by the UN General Assembly for the Year. Actions with the agencies of the UN family needed to be harmonized in a properly coordinated manner for effectiveness.

Writing for the UN required a unique style. So I familiarized myself with the guidelines of the correspondence manual. My letters were concisely constructed, with the main reasons for writing clearly spelled out in the introductory section. The rest of the content set out the details in constructive, diplomatic language. Expedient messages were customarily written in a telegraphic style and transmitted by facsimile.

Like every office of the UN, the Centre for Social Development and Humanitarian Affairs (CSDHA) had a rigid hierarchical order of staff and responsibility. Each document I wrote was routinely screened at the various hierarchical levels. This was called 'clearance procedure' in the UN administrative language. Depending on their degree of importance, all the documents were cleared in turn by my immediate supervisor, the chief of unit, the deputy-director of the branch, the director of the division, the assistant secretary-general of the centre, and then the director-general of the UN office at Vienna.

I quickly became accustomed to the reality that it must take a while for the documents written by me to be approved, signed, and dispatched to their destinations. In many instances, the corrections were not of substance, but addressed editorial issues and style. This experience was not limited to me alone as an individual staff member. It was part and parcel of the culture of the organization.

For example, the Advisory Committee on IYDP reported to the Commission on Social Development; the commission reported to the Economic and Social Council; and the council reported to the General Assembly. Each of the documents emanating from those levels was labelled 'Report of the Secretary-General' and was submitted to the General Assembly for approval and adoption.

I never doubted the efficiency and effectiveness of the organization and its bureaucracy. Like most young people of my time, I esteemed the UN and was highly attracted to it. Its mission of peace, development, justice, and freedom fascinated my imagination. So the opportunity to be part of the UN and to contribute to its mission was prestigious and a big morale booster for me.

I was now firmly established in the Secretariat, and the office work became a simple routine. Ingo, too, was in total control, and the responsibility of guiding and protecting me became a simple daily routine. Depending upon what clothing I was (or was not!) putting on and the time of the day, Ingo knew exactly what activity we were about to undertake, and he adjusted himself for action accordingly.

If I were in the street walking along the pavement to a destination totally unknown to me, I would ask someone to describe the way to me. I would then pass on this information to Ingo through the appropriate commands, and he would execute the instructions accordingly.

'Forward!' I would say, and he would guide me straight until we arrived at the road junction. Then he would stop and wait, expecting to hear one of a series of commands, out of which only one could apply: 'To the left', 'To the right',

'Watch the cars', 'Cross the road', 'About turn left', or 'About turn right'.

If we needed to cross two junctions before turning left into the street at the next crossroads, I would instruct Ingo to watch out for the moving cars and cross the street straight to the kerb. We would then continue heading forward on our journey. On arrival, I would instruct Ingo to 'Find door left', and he would nuzzle up to show me the door handle. Inside the building, I would ask him to find the lift or the staircase. So, finally, we would arrive at our destination. We applied the same procedure in our daily journeys to and from the office. But after a second journey on the same route, Ingo no longer needed the spoken commands anymore as he superbly navigated the way on his own independently, and, very often, to the astonishment of other pedestrians.

As a gesture of goodwill, the city of Vienna initially provided a shuttle bus service to facilitate transportation of UN staff to the newly opened Vienna International Centre, popularly known by the Viennese as the 'UNO-City', located on the other side of the Danube River. Several bus stops were arranged across the city for UN staff members that opted to use the service.

This was very convenient for me since I was living with my family in the Hagenmüllergasse 23 in the third district of Vienna and very close to one of the VIC shuttle bus stops. All I needed to do every morning was to walk down our street with Ingo to the Danube Canal and upstream to the nearest VIC shuttle bus stop in the Wassergasse. The bus took us, along with other commuters, to the VIC and into the building.

If I missed the VIC shuttle bus, I alternatively took the tram from the Erdbergstrasse to the Landstrasse, then another tram or the fast train (*Schnellbahn*) to the Praterstern station, and another tram to the Vienna International Centre.

We repeated this procedure in reverse every evening at the end of the working day in our return journeys.

Surely, I understood that life was a global theatre in which everyone was on the stage. I was also conscious of the reality that I had a unique act to perform, which destiny had bestowed on me. I was determined to play that role to the best of my ability. My guide dog helped me in a big way to minimize that stigma of helplessness when I was in the public. Blindness was no longer a reason for people to pity me. They were no longer insecure with me in the street; instead, I was making more contacts with them in my daily journeys to and from work. With my guide dog, I was master of my destiny in a respectful way.

I once asked my wife Renate, why people behaved the way they did to me in the public. She said, 'You embody too many impressions on one spot at a time. You are working with a guide dog, which in itself is a unique experience and very seldom in the city. The dog is beautiful and well maintained. You are blind and a black man, meticulously dressed up. You speak fluent German and always in a business-like manner. You are cheerful and friendly. Together, you and your guide dog exhibit a positive image of life.'

With all that in mind, one day on our way home after work, I got off the tram at the Praterstern station to catch the fast train. It was rush hour, and commuters were moving in all directions. Suddenly, I noticed a man walking beside me. He asked me in a friendly voice, 'Is your dog blind?' I instantly replied, 'Yes, surely. Can't you see me guiding him?' But, to my surprise, before I could slow down my paces to give him a more logical explanation of the matter, I found he had quickly disappeared with the wind.

Sometimes, I went to schools and kindergartens in my free time from work, and told young students the story of my life, and some exciting African fairy tales. One morning, as

I was travelling to work, a little boy entered the train with an old man. On seeing my guide dog, and me, the little boy said loudly to the old man, 'Grandpa, that is the fairy uncle from Africa!' I smiled at the little boy, and greeted him very friendly. The old man told me that he was taking him to the kindergarten, where I had been recently.

My first UN mission abroad was to Tokyo to attend the first International Abilympics, which was organized to commemorate the 1981 International Year of Disabled Persons. I accompanied the assistant secretary-general and head of the Centre for Social Development and Humanitarian Affairs to represent the UN.

The trip lasted ten days, and, for the first time, I travelled without my guide dog. It was not necessary to take Ingo along with me. The organizers of the event in Japan had generously undertaken to provide me with a car and a driver, a human guide, and an interpreter in the local language. I gladly welcomed this arrangement since Ingo and I were consequently spared unavoidable stressful situations such as the long air travel from Europe. So I could relax and concentrate fully on my various assignments at the event.

But before embarking on the trip, I, as a typhlonaut (a blind, but skilfully mobile, traveller), needed every detail to be organized. Renate was very instrumental in the process. She sorted my clothing—shirts, suits, ties, and socks—into sets and arranged them in perfectly matching order. I labelled them all in Braille accordingly. In a separate Braille notebook, I systematically described each item in all the sets, so that I could always be sure that my clothing matched. It was a precautionary measure, so as to avoid muddling up the order of the sets when I unpacked the suitcase.

Our flight was with KLM Royal Dutch Airlines via Amsterdam and Ankridge, to Narita International Airport in Tokyo. On arrival, our hosts were promptly on hand at the airport to welcome us. The assistant secretary-general and I were driven in separate vehicles to the Kio Plaza Hotel in the centre of the city. After completing registration formalities at the hotel reception desk, I was assisted by my guide and interpreter to my room.

While in the room, I applied the principle 'Be organized; pay attention to details'. So I asked my guide to walk me through all the strategic items in the room. I noted the on and off positions of the switches, which was especially important so I could control the lights in the room at all times. In the bathroom, I located the outlet for the electric shaver on the wall, and studied the system of mixing cold and hot water for shower, bath, and sink.

On the telephone equipment, I memorized important extensions so I could make calls, especially with the reception desk for help. I explored the TV remote control equipment and buttons, the window curtains, and blinds. I carefully marked the door to the corridor by hanging my white cane on the door handle so I would not confuse it with the door to the bathroom. Finally, I located the refrigerator, my reading table and chair, and my bed.

The Abilympics movement was founded in the 1970s in Japan, and, in 1972, the Japan Association for Employment of the Handicapped organized the Olympics of Abilities. The aim was to promote the vocational skills of disabled persons and to encourage them to participate actively in the labour market.

Similarly, the activities of the 1981 International Abilympics were organized in categories of work skills, workshops, and conferences. In the work skills category, the participants had the opportunity to demonstrate their level of workmanship in an open, international competition with disabled persons from other countries. The final results were determined on the quality of the performance of the individual competitors in the various disciplines.

I visited each of the many pavilions and witnessed the individual competitors exhibit their work skills. But I was more involved in the different workshops and conferences, as well as attending the opening and closing ceremonies, where I sat next to the assistant secretary-general in the arena at the head of the UN delegation. We conducted a number of press briefings separately before and after each activity, in which I gave interviews to journalists.

I took part in one of the panel discussions and made a presentation on my 'Experiences Working for the UN as a Visually Impaired Person'. I was featured on local radio and television programmes and in newspapers, which made many people remember the articles they had read about my guide dog and me in Vienna. Many of my fellow blind participants from Japan were very impressed. A typical complimentary comment was, 'You work for the UN? You must be the cleverest blind man in the world.'

My daily routine was strictly limited to moving between the locations of the various work skills competitions, conferences, and workshops. But I took the opportunity of a half-day off given to the participants to relax and explore the city of Tokyo, though in a very limited circumstance because of time constraints. I visited some historic sites, including temples where one could buy little bells called 'good luck charms'. These were extremely popular with the ladies in Tokyo, I especially observed. They attach the 'good luck charms' to their bracelets and handbags. This was a big advantage for me since I could easily identify the ladies passing by and around me at any time.

I cherished so much the generosity and friendship of our hosts that I managed to learn some expressions in Japanese through my guide. The time was short, and the event stressful but fulfilling. The time had come to leave Tokyo at the end of the first International Abilympics. At the airport, my guide passionately told me that there were two little beautiful and sad expressions in the Japanese language, which she would like to share with me. I was naturally curious to know these expressions. With her eyes full of tears, she embraced me and said, '*Arigato* and *Sayonara* ... thank you and goodbye.' Just as she was expressing, at that moment, I felt so happy and so sad to depart.

Back in Vienna, Renate brought our little daughter Esther and Ingo to meet me at the airport. Our return journey from Japan had lasted over thirty-six hours, instead of the usual seventeen hours, due to flight delays. Ingo was so excited that he ran and jumped over every object in the arrival area, forcing people to take cover as they would if they were in an air raid. He was out of control with joy, and acted as if he had not seen me for ten years rather than ten days. It took a while before he could calm down so I could greet my wife and my little daughter. For the next few days at home, he never moved too far from me, fearing that I might again disappear without him.

I returned to the office to observe increased activities on the name-amended International Year *of* Disabled Persons. Organizations of disabled persons themselves had mushroomed tremendously, and national committees had been established in many countries. These developments were systematically reflected in the reports of the Advisory Committee, the Interagency Meeting, the Commission on Social Development, and the Economic and Social Council to the General Assembly. The popular demand by organizations of disabled persons had led to replacing the preposition *for* with *of* in the title of IYDP.

The overriding objective of the Year was to develop a

blueprint document for action in the field of disability. But it was soon realized that this ambitious project could not be completed in one year alone. So the General Assembly decided to extend IYDP into 1992 to provide more time to complete the work on the elaboration of a world plan of action.

My initial work contract in October 1980 was fixed for a probationary period of three months, to be renewed for another nine months till the end of 1981. As the observance of IYDP extended into 1982, the contract was renewed accordingly, giving me the opportunity to continue with my contributions. However, these extensions did not occur without a price. With the limited number of accessible office tools at my disposal, I had to invest quadruple the time and energy that my sighted colleagues had to invest to produce and deliver equal work outputs.

Each contract extension in the Secretariat depended on a satisfactory performance of assigned duties, which I always mastered superbly to the astonishment of my colleagues. CSDHA was an out duty station of the Department of International Economic and Social Affairs (DIESA), based at the UN Headquarters in New York. All personnel and administrative actions in Vienna had to be approved by New York before they could be implemented. In many instances, the approvals were not obtained in a timely manner due to the physical distance between New York and Vienna, which very often caused me unpalatable anxieties and frustrations.

In 1982, I experienced a significant change in my train connection in my daily journeys to work. The underground train line was extended to the terminus Zentrum Kagran, with a stopover at the Vienna International Centre. The VIC shuttle bus service ceased to run through the area of the city in which I lived, and the tram from our home was replaced with the bus that ran between Stadionbrücke and the Landstrasse.

But Ingo quickly adjusted to the new routine, as we took the bus to connect to the underground train at the Landstrasse. Luckily, a group of colleagues from all the organizations in the VIC generously organized themselves in a car pool to drive me and my guide dog to and from work whenever necessary. I availed myself of this service only occasionally.

Ingo had a good sense of duty and tolerated no nonsense. One morning, we rushed up the street to catch the bus as it pulled into the station. We arrived late, the platform was very crowded, and the door shut right in front of Ingo's nose. I felt that he was deeply disappointed. Indeed, we had actually missed the bus because the other passengers had blocked our way to the door. The next morning, as we waited at the bus stop, Ingo sighted the bus at the traffic light across the road. As the bus pulled into the station, he raised his voice and barked to the left and to the right. Everyone jumped back and was shaken, but the way to the bus was immediately cleared of people. He majestically guided me into the bus, and swiftly turned round twinkling an eye as if to say, 'Okay, folks, now come in on board, if you wish!' From then on, each morning, whenever the bus pulled into the station, I would hear people say to one another respectfully, 'Let the dog and his master enter first!'

My work in the office was further boosted by the extension of IYDP when on 3 December 1982, the General Assembly adopted the World Programme of Action, and proclaimed the period 1983 to 1992 as the UN Decade of Disabled Persons. It was expected that the Decade would provide a practical time frame for the implementation of the World Programme of Action at the national, regional, and international levels. The Assembly also designated 3 December each year as the International Day on Disability to help keep the subject alive on the global agenda.

I was fully involved on equal footing with my colleagues in drawing up the World Programme of Action by collecting, analyzing, and compiling information based on the experience of IYDP. In the division of labour among the professional staff, I assumed the responsibility of researching, writing up, and presenting information on accessing environments, accessing information, developing organizations of disabled persons, and informing national disability committees.

But my work became more complex with the new division of labour, which focused mainly on finalizing the World Programme of Action and monitoring its implementation during the Decade of Disabled Persons. My working tools to date, which were limited to the Optacon, a tape recorder, and a Perkins Brailler machine, supplemented by volunteer readers and the secretary as amanuensis, were no longer sufficient. I could not meet the new challenges.

The latest progress in electronic communications technology made it possible for another exciting new product to be developed for the blind. The VersaBraille device was introduced to the market as one of the greatest advances in the history of Braille use. I grabbed the opportunity and immediately purchased one. I was excited when a representative of the local marketing company delivered the equipment to me in the office. But I was initially cautious not to exaggerate my excitement, given my adventurous experience with the Optacon.

Until now, one of the biggest handicaps for me had been my inability to edit independently the documents I produced with the Perkins Braille machine and the normal typewriter. But the VersaBraille device came with a Perkins type-six Braille keyboard, a space bar, and several other function keys. Its most innovative technology was the twenty-cell, refreshable Braille line (display) and the text advance control bar. With the Braille keys, I typed the text onto a high-quality cassette tape, instead of paper, and the characters appeared simultaneously on the twenty-cell, refreshable Braille line for me to read and control.

I was introduced to the field of computer technology through the use of a number of software that enabled the VersaBraille to interact with other devices. For the first time, I was able to create a readable text printout of a text prepared in Braille, which was a great boost to my writing productivity and efficiency, and eliminated the need for me to transcribe and translate texts into Braille and then dictate them into a tape recorder. I edited the texts directly using the VersaBraille editor, and printed the texts out on a dot matrix printer.

Additional software that interacted with the VersaBraille enabled me to view the texts from other devices on the refreshable Braille display a line at a time, such as in a Teletype. It was an immense advancement for me, as I finally had the opportunity to interface my computer workstation with the Wang Office Operating System, like everyone else among the staff.

Now, fully equipped with the new technology, I felt less stress as I carried out my complex assignments. My fields of responsibility for implementing the World Programme of Action focused naturally on access to the physical environment, information materials, and promoting organizations of disabled persons. One of my main challenges was to figure out how to make at least some of the important information materials available in formats that were accessible to the blind. In many developed countries, such materials were already produced in accessible formats, though to a relatively limited degree. But, in the developing countries, the blind did not have anything close to the same opportunity their peers in the developed countries had.

The only option available to me was to organize into Braille and audio recordings the news from the IYDP Secretariat, the 'Circular Letter to the National Coordinating Committees', and the World Programme of Action Concerning Disabled Persons. In order to produce these materials in accessible formats, I skilfully negotiated with benevolent organizations and institutions in Germany, the United States of America, the United Kingdom of Great Britain, and Austria. The circulation to the recipients worldwide was simple and straightforward since I utilized the normal UN mail operation facility for the purpose. But my success to provide this service was largely on a small scale as a result of financial constraints and logistic limitations.

The UN premises must be accessible to disabled persons at all times. I probably understood this problem better than anyone else since I was a member of the staff and a disabled person myself. I consequently became a point of reference and quasi expert on the subject in the Secretariat. I took advantage of my situation and very quickly set myself at work on the matter at all levels.

It was universally assumed that the UN must live by example when it came to accessibility of its physical environment to disabled persons. A number of the participants at the meetings of the Commission on Social Development, the Advisory Committee on IYDP, and the Ad Hoc Interagency Meeting, held annually at the Vienna International Centre, were disabled persons themselves. It was, therefore, imperative that the physical environment of the Vienna International Centre building be made accessible to them so as to enhance their active participation and make sure their contributions were on equal footing with those of other participants.

I carried out an in-depth investigation of the accessibility requirements of the VIC building, drawing up a master plan and practical recommendations for urgent improvements. The VIC Buildings Management implemented some of the measures I recommended. Ramps were constructed to enhance access for wheelchair users into the building, and special areas were designated in the cafeteria for disabled guests. But Buildings Management did not implement a number of other measures I recommended due mainly to technical and financial constraints. Some of these measures would have required the installation of unique audio signals and announcements and Braille markings in the lifts to identify the different floor levels.

The issue of access to the physical environment was receiving increased attention worldwide. So I travelled to Switzerland to investigate the accessibility of the physical environment of the UN office at Geneva. While in Geneva, I conducted a series of interviews with key staff members of the Buildings Management section, as well as with a number of disabled persons who worked in the building. I received a report from the Buildings Management of the UN Headquarters in New York on the accessibility of the building there.

I analyzed the results of these investigations and wrote a comprehensive report with far-reaching recommendations on how to make the UN buildings and information facilities in Vienna, Geneva, and New York accessible to disabled persons. For years, the report continued to be an invaluable source of reference to the respective buildings management sections for implementing actions on 'accessible UN premises'.

I fairly understood that the effort of the UN on accessibility could not be limited to its premises alone. So

I supervised the commissioning of renowned experts to conduct a series of studies, which resulted in the issuance of technical publications to serve as guidelines to governments, policy makers, architects, designers, and members of the general public. Among these was 'Designing with Care: A Guide to Adaptation of the Built Environment for Disabled Persons', which was undertaken in collaboration with the Swedish International Development Authority and the UN Environment Programme.

The VersaBraille equipment was portable, compact, and immensely convenient. I carried it with me wherever I went. The written documents that I required were all comfortably stored on the electronic magnetic cassette tapes. I read out my speeches and interventions to the audience directly from the Braille display, took notes, and rehearsed them instantly on the spot. What a glorious relief! This was crucial in my official travels when I actively participated and delivered speeches personally at national, regional, and international events. If the exigencies of duty did not permit me to travel, I wrote the appropriate statement, which was transmitted to the participants or delivered in person by a representative of the UN at the event.

The resources of the trust fund established by the General Assembly for the IYDP were used to attend to requests for assistance from developing countries and organizations of disabled persons and to further the implementation of the World Programme of Action. The West African Federation of Organizations of Disabled Persons was one of the regional networks in the developing countries to receive financial support from the IYDP trust fund. The federation held two leadership training seminars for its member organizations in Dakar, Senegal, in December 1982, and in Nouakchott, Mauritania, in February 1985 respectively. Most of the participating organizations were from West African French–

speaking countries. I attended the two events to represent the UN.

Although the two leadership seminars were held at different times and at different locations, the messages I brought from Vienna to the participants on both occasions were identical in content. The messages stressed encouragement and self-evaluation.

The training seminars were organized in plenary sessions and workshops in which political and general statements were made, as well as presentations on the outcome of the workshops. Training modules covered how to establish and run an organization. I utilized both platforms to familiarize the participants with the stipulations of the World Programme of Action Concerning Disabled Persons.

As I arrived to attend the leadership training seminar, the minister of social affairs of Senegal met me at the Dakar International Airport. He accompanied me in his official limousine to the hotel where I was provided accommodation. My local guides told me that there was uncertainty among the people as to my actual origin. Some people thought I was a Black American. Others disputed this speculation, drawing attention to my distinct Black African features. They could not imagine how a blind African could be working for the UN and occupying my position and travelling around the world to represent the organization. As happened in Tokyo the previous year, my peers in Dakar were full of admiration of me, and I felt very honoured to be among them and to encourage them in their struggle for recognition, equality, and full participation in their society.

On our free day during the training seminar, we went on an excursion by ship to Goree Island, the most famous favourite tourist attraction in Senegal. We were taken on a guided toured of the Slave House, one of the most frequently visited sites on the island. Our guide told us that Slave

House was a reminder of the island's role as the centre of the West African slave trade. Built by the Dutch in 1776, the Slave House has been preserved in its original state. It was one of the several sites on the island where the African slaves were brought to the 'door of no return' to be loaded onto ships bound for the New World. The slave owners' residential quarters were on the upper floor. The lower floor was reserved for the slaves, who were weighed, fed, and held before departing on the transatlantic journey. Thousands of tourists like us visited the Slave House each year.

The people in our group were horrified at the architecture of the Slave House. I even heard some American female tourists weeping loudly. The guide reminded us that our African and European ancestors alike committed this crime against humanity. He said that, if an apology or reparation was required for this inhumanity, today's descendants of Africans and Europeans must make it equally. I listened soberly to the guide's narration of the history of the slave trade, and was so sickened and upset that I did not have any appetite for the meal we were served when we went back to the ship for our return trip to Dakar.

As it had been in Dakar, when I arrived in Nouakchott to attend the second leadership training seminar in February 1985, I was welcomed at the airport by the Mauritanian minister of social affairs. He accompanied me in his official limousine to my accommodation in a workers' hostel in the outskirts of the city. The organizers of the seminar had rented the hostel to accommodate all the participants. The rooms were built in self-contained apartments. I was booked into two of these apartments. I used one as my sleeping room and the other as a meeting room for receiving and consulting with the delegates of other organizations attending the seminar. I made sure that my guide described the location of all the facilities in the rooms to me before he left me on my own.

I settled down in the rooms and unpacked my suitcase. The minister was giving a reception in the main hall of the hostel that evening to welcome the participants. Before changing clothes for the occasion, I went quickly to the bathroom to have a shower. As I opened the tap, instead of running water, a series of air explosions gushed out. I jumped back and was tremendously scared. I thought I might have running water in the second bathroom, but I found out that the situation was no different there. I rushed to the telephone to call the reception desk for help. When I lifted up the receiver, I heard no signals. I experienced the same scenario with the telephone in the second room.

I instantly walked out to the corridor only to find another totally blind participant who had just had a similar experience in his room. We stood there completely at a loss, expecting some sighted individual to pass by. Word finally got to the reception desk about our ordeal. We were told that the generator for the water pump was out of order but would be operating again in thirty minutes. I did not attend the reception because water only began running from the tap shortly before midnight. Apologies were exchanged, and a system was devised for tap water rationing for participants in the hostel.

We all adhered to the prescribed schedule for using the water; however, when all the people turned all the taps on at the same time, the pump pressure became too weak to bring the water up to the taps. I was privileged to have two bathrooms, and was also supplied with buckets. When the taps were closed and there was low demand, I filled out the baths and buckets with water. By so doing, I had water available at all times. It was a memorable occasion for me to experience life in a Sahel Zone and to witness the ingenuity of the people who had to survive in such an environment.

(The Sahel Zone is the savannah that lies directly south of the Sahara Desert.)

I represented the UN at the European Seminar on the Accessibility of Public Buildings and Facilities for the Disabled (Utrecht, Netherlands, October 1987) and the Seminar on Building Adaptable Houses (Nunspeet, Netherlands, May/June 1989) organized by the Commission for the European Communities, as well as the Second International Seminar on Creating Non-handicapping Environment – Renewal of Inner Cities (Prague, Czechoslovakia, October 1987), organized by the International Council for building Research Studies and Documentation. The most significant result of these gatherings was the formulation of policy directives to ensure accessible environment to all members of society, including disabled persons.

I particularly enjoyed my address to the participants at the European Conference on New Forms for Vocational Integration for Disabled People, held in Lisbon, Portugal, in November 1988. The topic of the conference was closely related to my special circumstances and career development at the UN. So the approach in my speech was exceptionally inspiring. I acquainted the participants with the mandates of Centre for Social Development and Humanitarian Affairs as the source of my authority, and explained to them the aims and objectives of the World Programme of Action Concerning Disabled Persons.

Mindful of my own circumstances, I told the participants that the UN had taken concrete steps to promote equal employment opportunities for disabled persons within its various programmes and activities. A policy statement adopted by the Administrative Committee on Coordination had set forth a range of statutory provisions to enhance equal employment opportunities for disabled persons within the UN system.

Armed with the authority of the UN, I concluded my speech with a rational demand and a philosophical lecture and said that, as we moved into the twenty-first century, it would be necessary for us to analyze the employment opportunities for the population at large and disabled persons in particular. By so doing, we would be able to ascertain the skills needed to meet the requirements of the changing job market in view of recent trends in employment opportunities.

In my relatively short period of employment with the UN, I had, by default, become an international icon in the field of disability. I was not only recognized in the Secretariat but in the entire UN system and beyond as the symbol of equal employment opportunity for disabled persons. The Vienna office was highly commended for its enviable accomplishment in helping to implement the UN-declared policy on the employment of disabled persons.

I was 'exploited and paraded' at meetings and public events to show that the UN was living up to its expectations. At meetings, representatives of governments, agencies of the UN family, and non-governmental organizations were constantly astonished when they realized that I was an equal member of the staff of the Secretariat. Naturally, I was fully aware of this potential and my usefulness to the organization.

I was quite happily enjoying the universal recognition of my individual accomplishments. The only fly in the ointment was the ambiguous and chilly working relation with the chief of my unit. Since we first met, he had shown a cold shoulder to me, but he could not avoid our working together. I was somewhat surprised at his behaviour because, as a senior rehabilitation specialist, he was supposed to be accustomed to working with disabled persons. He was so mean and unfriendly to me that I could not please him.

He always found unnecessary faults with whatever I did even though my performance was highly acclaimed by other members of the staff. I initially accepted his behaviour as a sort of constructive criticism meant to improve the quality of our work. But soon I realized that there was more to it than met the eye. So I decided to find out the reason for his antagonistic behaviour towards me.

It would be presumptuous of me to expect everyone to embrace wholeheartedly my suddenly acquired iconic position in the field of disability. So I concluded—rightly or wrongly—that my chief of unit could not be immune to jealousy towards me, since this was one of the many weaknesses of mankind. I carefully investigated this phenomenon and found out that his apathy towards me was based on two pillars. First, I was apparently overshadowing him with my growing popularity, as people at times inadvertently referred to me as the chief of the unit. Second, he had voted against my recruitment, but the recruitment panel had rejected his preferred candidate. And he did not forgive me for that! I therefore adopted the olive branch approach in my working relationship with him.

I was fully aware that my workplace at the UN was not a sheltered workshop. It was an open and highly competitive working environment. I was not in any way or at any time naive and could not take any chances. I remained vigilant and constantly quadruplicated my effort to protect my job. All eyes were focused on me. I was scrutinized on every detail. Having an obnoxious chief constantly on my back only added to the pressure. I was not only challenged to perform my assigned duties over and above satisfaction, but I had to skilfully manage and control the enormous stress and work pressure without showing any signs of diminishing energy and strength.

I invited the chief of my unit and his wife to our home for a dinner, not so much as a favour to him, but more to establish a kind of *entente cordiale* in our embattled relations. He came with his wife on the agreed day on a weekend. When they entered the antechamber of our flat, they were offered guest shoes as was our custom. My chief of unit was furious and stubbornly refused to change his shoes. My wife explained to him politely that our little baby girl, Jacqueline, who was our second daughter, was crawling all over the flat on the floor.

When he finally submitted to the request, we noticed that the soles of his shoes were very dirty and unbearably stinking. He had obviously stepped into a freshly heaped dog's mess on the street before entering our building complex. My wife quickly took the shoes out of the flat and cleaned them in the corridor. My wife and I were shocked and astonished at his behaviour because, as a Dane and a middle European, he should be naturally aware of the hygiene and health risks involved in the situation. Yet he considered the occurrence as a snub and did not forgive me for it long thereafter!

I observed that, at the UN, there were two reasons that could lead to losing one's job. It could either be sustained poor performance of duty or covert intrigues, maliciously plotted by someone else against you. Certainly, the chief of my unit had chosen the later option—plus cynicism—as he was determined to get me kicked out of the UN as soon as he could.

This was bizarre and somewhat paradoxical as it was a European who had rescued me from the imminent hell of death in the battlefield in Biafra, the south-eastern province of Nigeria, which seceded after the federal military government had contemptuously subverted and repudiated the peace agreement that was reached at a meeting held in Aburi, Ghana, from 4 to 5 January 1967. These acts precipitated the Nigerian Civil War. But here was another European acting totally in a different direction. He was determined, without mercy, to cut off my umbilical cord and deprive me of the essence of my livelihood.

Periodic evaluation reports were regularly conducted on the performance of the individual staff members. The chief of my unit had chosen this medium to inflict unwarranted maximum damage on my reputation. He deliberately inserted a negative phrase in the supervisor's section of my performance evaluation reports. I refused to accept it and protested vehemently against the injustice.

I took the matter to the UN office at Vienna Rebuttal Panel, which was one of the Secretariat's administrative justice mechanisms. Its membership was made up of staff and administration representatives. The panel conducted an in-depth investigation of my complaint and found no grounds for a negative appraisal of my performance. I was exonerated and won the case convincingly. The chief of my unit was commanded to retract the negative phrase in my performance evaluation report. He was infuriated, but had to comply with the decision of the panel.

In the meantime, I received a letter from United Nations Educational, Scientific and Cultural Organization (UNESCO) in Paris for an interview in response to my application for the job of the managing editor of the *UNESCO Braille Courier*. The magazine was published quarterly in English, French, Spanish, and Korean. The information published in the magazine was taken from the printed edition of the *UNESCO Courier* and from other UN publications.

I travelled to Paris and had a very successful interview for the job at UNESCO headquarters, and was introduced to my prospective new working environment. I was full of optimism when I returned back to Vienna after the interview.

In the following weeks, as part of the preparations for my prospective new job, I underwent a series of official medical tests, which were carried out at the VIC medical unit on behalf of UNESCO. But, as I waited to receive the letter of my appointment, UNESCO suddenly plunged into a deep financial crisis.

A number of its major financial contributors, like the United States of America and the United Kingdom of Great Britain, suspended their membership of the organization. UNESCO was forced to freeze some of its programmes, and my prospective new job with the organization was affected.

My contractual status had been extremely unstable since the IYDP and continued that way well into the Decade of Disabled Persons. The post I occupied was funded through extra-budgetary resources. At times, my contract was extended only for a few months. This was a convenient weapon at the hand of the chief of my unit to effectively destroy me. I was later told that, in a staff meeting, he succeeded in convincing the assistant secretary-general to send a confidential interoffice memorandum to the executive office of Department of International Economic and Social Affairs (DIESA) at UN Headquarters in New York, recommending that my contract be terminated when it expired on 15 May 1985 for lack of resources, although there was no lack.

The memorandum and its content caused consternation at the executive office in New York, I discovered later, as they could make neither head nor tail of such a decision from Vienna. The DIESA could not afford to lose an important icon like me in the UN programme on disability at that crucial period. So the executive office quickly investigated the matter by wires and overruled the decision of the Vienna office.

The executive office dispatched an immediate memorandum by cable to the assistant secretary-general in

Vienna, instructing that my contract be extended for two years against a regular budget post, which had been directly identified from New York. What a blessing in disguise! The order from the executive office set off shock waves in Vienna. The chief of my unit was deeply struck, but was definitely comforted by his regular mandatory retirement six weeks afterwards. Surely, honesty is the head that wears the crown!

My guide dog and I had become an institution in the Vienna International Centre. Ingo, especially, was admired and respected, and we had made a lot of friends in the building. Unfortunately, Ingo had recently developed serious health problems, the gravity of which we were not aware of when the symptoms first appeared. In June 1986, he was suddenly diagnosed with cancer in the lymph glands. The illness was discovered too late for any reasonable therapeutic intervention.

The cancer was in a very advanced stage, and there were already metastases all over Ingo's body. The veterinary surgeon informed me that Ingo would live for only a few more weeks. I was shocked and devastated by the news, as I could not imagine life without Ingo. But Ingo braved the illness, to my astonishment, and never allowed it to deter him from guiding and helping me.

In the midst of worries about the rapidly deteriorating health condition of my guide dog, I received an invitation to attend a seminar dealing with the education, training, and employment of disabled persons in the United Kingdom of Great Britain. The Royal Society for the Blind organized the event at its headquarters in Dorton Manor House in Seal, near Sevenoaks in Kent, England. The Royal London Society for the Blind was established in 1838 primarily for bringing literacy to the blind. But in addition to its educational activities, the society opened its first workshop in 1888 to provide visually impaired people with new training and employment opportunities. It was therefore imperative for the UN to participate in the event to provide moral support and to exchange knowledge and experience with specialists in the field.

In preparing for the mission, I carefully revisited all my habitual typhlonautic travelling procedures. My suits, shirts, and ties were arranged and labelled in Braille according to matching colours and fashion in the suitcase. Before leaving the flat, I squatted on the floor in the antechamber and went through all the items in the suitcase and the hand luggage to ascertain that everything was in place. Renate and Jacqueline and my ailing guide dog accompanied me to the airport in our family car. Our journey was unnerving and strenuous due to heavy traffic and sudden road diversions. We arrived at the airport just in time for me to catch my flight.

At the check-in counter, the airline personnel had information in advance about my special requirements for the flight. My luggage was swiftly checked in. A staff member of the airline was charged to help me go through the customs and security procedures and get onto to the plane. I was accustomed to this kind of treatment and support by the airlines at all airports around the globe. These services made things a lot easier for me to travel independently at all times. I always accepted the offer to sit in a wheelchair. This was not because I was too frail to walk. I simply did not want to overburden my escort in guiding me, carrying my heavy hand luggage, and walking the notorious long distances at the airports. I sat comfortably in the wheel chair with the hand luggage resting on my lap, and my escort pushed me from behind for easy and fast navigation.

I sat on the plane in the business class section elegantly dressed in a nice suit and tie. My appearance was that of an international civil servant on a business trip. Before our plane lifted off from the ground, I introduced myself to the traveller sitting next to me. I always did so on flights in order to mobilize help in addition to the aid given to me by the stewardess on board. We were soon engaged in a friendly and spirited conversation, in which we shared information about our occupations in relation to our current business trip.

Shortly after the meals were served, the stewardess returned to take orders for drinks. As if I should do justice to my noble status as an international civil servant, I proudly ordered myself a bottle of French champagne. I had almost consumed half of the champagne when the stewardess appeared to collect the payment. I went for my wallet in my jacket pocket. It was not there. I searched for it in my hand luggage; it was not there, either. I turned the hand luggage and everything else upside down. My wallet was nowhere to be found. I was nervous, sweating, and frightened. I had no money to pay for the exorbitant drink that I had so proudly purchased.

When the news got to the captain, he came to me to find out the true story himself. 'What's the matter, Mr. Eze?' I explained that I could not pay for the drink because my wallet was missing. He was very sympathetic and believed my story. He said, 'Don't worry, Mr. Eze. Please accept the champagne with my compliments. Thanks for flying British Airways. We hope to see you again!' He concluded and patted me on the shoulder and walked back to the cockpit. While I appreciated the generous treat to free French champagne by the captain as a great relief, it helped me only to solve a part of the problem. My participation at the seminar would last for the whole week, and I needed money for my subsistence during the trip. I was anxious and restless throughout the flight. I could not comprehend how my safely secured wallet came to be missing in a broad daylight. Could I have become a victim of an unfortunate theft at the airport? I nervously finished consuming the rest of the champagne and sank into a deep thought.

When we finally landed in London at Heathrow Airport, I immediately telephoned my wife in Vienna from the British Airways office. She told me that, when she returned from the airport and entered the flat, she found my wallet lying on the floor in the antechamber. It was on the very spot where I had squatted down to go through the contents of my suitcase before departing for the airport.

She immediately went to the post office to remit money to me at my address in England, but she was informed that the Austrian post office had stopped monetary transmission and delivery services to the United Kingdom only a few weeks before. If she remitted the money through the bank, it would take about a week to reach me in England, by which time the seminar would have been concluded. I was therefore obliged to borrow money from the Royal London Society for the Blind for my daily subsistence, which I repaid through a bank transaction immediately on my return to Austria.

At the end of the seminar in Sevenoaks, I travelled by train to visit my English friend Liz and her family in Tiverton, Devon. We had first met in Austria and became friends when we participated in an international Red Cross summer youth camp, which was organized by the Austrian Red Cross Society in 1971. We strictly maintained our friendship by exchanging regular Christmas greeting cards and family visits. During my present visit, we were even featured in one of the local newspapers as an example of a genuine friendship between people of different races.

After spending the weekend in Tiverton, I travelled by train from Exeter back to London. I had to change trains in Reading to travel to Heathrow airport for my return flight to Vienna. I now experienced English humour first hand on the ground. The British Rails Authority had assigned one of its personnel to assist me at Reading station. When our train arrived from Exeter, the gentleman met me on the platform. He carried my luggage in a trolley, and I walked beside him, my hand on his shoulder. I was elegantly dressed in my international civil servant attire. When we entered the lift, I remarked in an impressed way that it was a huge conveyance. The gentleman responded politely in a typical London accent, 'Yes, sir. You are a big man!' But I later realized that he had taken me on a freight elevator. Then I had the privilege of enjoying English generosity in the form of yet another free treat to French champagne by the captain on the plane.

I returned to Vienna to my guide dog Ingo. I was so sad he could not come with my family to the airport to welcome me home. His terminal illness had finally slowed him down. When I entered the flat, he painstakingly came to greet me. He could neither drink nor eat. He could no longer bark, and the whole Monday night, he breathed heavily and sparingly. The veterinary surgeon could help him no more to stay alive. The following afternoon, Tuesday, 12 July 1986, my guide dog, sadly, passed away. I was traumatized and devastated. A long mourning period had begun for me before I knew it. The news of Ingo's death was received with sympathy in the entire Vienna International Centre. A eulogy was published in the next issuances of all the staff journals of the Vienna-based organizations in memory of Ingo's passing away for all time.

Life was strange and hollow without Ingo, both at home and at work. I could not relieve my deep mourning for his loss; it was going to last for a lifetime. People constantly enquired about my guide dog wherever I went as they were only used to seeing me on six legs. People were sympathetic, and they joined in my sorrow when they learned about Ingo's passing away. I was subsequently bombarded with questions, such as How are you going to manage without your dog? Are you going to get another dog? Many of them even offered me their assistance, which they correctly assumed I badly needed in such a horrible situation.

I was terrified to learn that I would not be getting a replacement for Ingo so soon. The guide dog school in Germany informed me that it would take at least ten months to train another dog for me. 'What a long time to wait in my situation!' I exclaimed. I heard about a guide dog trainer from the United States of America. He trained his dogs in Hollywood, California, and flew over with them to Hamburg, Germany. I travelled with my wife and my younger daughter to Hamburg to meet the trainer and to examine his dogs. But I found his method of training tedious and impractical, as it would have obliged me to stay in his training camp in Hamburg for four weeks. We returned to Vienna with an unaccomplished mission and without a guide dog.

While I waited for a guide dog to be trained for me, I turned to the traditional 'snail move' in which I depended partly on the white cane for my mobility. But I was no longer used to a system that overtly slowed down my ability to get to a desired destination. With efficiency in mind, I adopted a system of 'relay move' in which sighted people assisted me from one strategic point along my desired destination to another. But, it was only a slight improvement of the snail move. It made me totally dependent on the goodwill of other people, which I appreciated despite the frustration and demoralization, as I had no choice. These two systems of mobility were no match to the 'fly move' in which my guide dog and I could walk swiftly on six legs to any destination in the world. With this system, I could accomplish twenty times as much activity as with my other mobility systems.

My wife drove me regularly in our family car to and from my work place. When she could not drive me, I utilized the car pool, which some colleagues at the Vienna International Centre had organized on my behalf. Once I entered my office and sat at my desk, I organized my mobility inside the building during the day. Depending on my schedule, I might need to go to the post office, commissary (duty-free shop for staff), different offices and conference and meeting rooms, bank, restaurant, and cafeteria. I might even want to go out to the Danube Park for a walk at lunchtime. So I would sit at the telephone for hours, calling around to arrange for assistance with any available colleague. It was a very frustrating experience since people had their own individual daily programme.

At times, I arranged for assistance, especially for lunch in the cafeteria or the restaurant, well in advance in order to avoid last-minute disappointment, which very often occurred. When that happened, I reluctantly resorted to snail move and proceeded to the corridor before someone came along to offer me help. My consolation was that this state of affairs was only temporary and that life would be back to normal in a few months when my guide dog arrived. It was also clear to me that this state of affairs would always occur whenever my guide dog was inhibited from duty as a consequence of an illness.

My work in the office had risen to a peak with the activities in preparation for the mid decade review of the implementation of the World Programme of Action. As the focal point on disability matters, our office prepared a monitoring questionnaire, which was distributed to governments of member states and organizations, requesting information on their compliance with the recommendations of the World Programme of Action. A flurry of activities ensued as the replies were received at our office, coupled with the extraordinary involvement of the inter-agency meeting and the Commission on social Development in the analysis process of the monitoring questionnaire. The major tasks in the office were equitably shared among the professional staff according to the individual's field of responsibility, in which I played an exceptional role.

As I struggled in frustration with the mobility to accomplish my tasks in the office, I received information from Germany that my guide dog had finished training and that she was ready for me. I was out of myself with joy by the news. In May 1987, I travelled to Germany by train to meet my new guide dog in the same school where Ingo was trained. My new friend was a female longhair German shepherd dog. She was very intelligent and extremely beautiful. The trainer introduced us to each other. Her name was Weka. We quickly became good friends after some initial caresses and nuzzles. I trained with her for a week in the school and travelled back with her to Vienna. My wife and daughters came to meet us at the railway station. Like other people we had met along our way, my family was very impressed by her outstanding beauty, especially because of her long hair.

The honeymoon with Weka did not last for long. Within a few days of settling down and working with her in Vienna, I discovered her peculiar idiosyncrasy—she had an impulsive fear of objects in the city, both animate and inanimate. She was afraid of lifts, telephone booths, large lorries, fast-moving objects, trams, and underground trains, not to mention crowds of people. While in harness and on duty, she would become hysterical and suddenly begin barking aggressively at people in all directions. I was scared and worried as I was unable to control her in these situations. I telephoned the trainer in Germany and told him about my unexpected problems with Weka. He was very surprised and said that Weka had never shown such behaviour throughout her period of training in the village. Otherwise, she would not have qualified as a professional guide dog from his school.

At the suggestion of my acquaintances who were long-time dog owners, I consulted a renowned veterinary surgeon and domestic animal psychologist in our neighbourhood regarding Weka's paranoia and strange behaviour. He prescribed a therapy which he believed would remedy the condition. It involved giving Weka a combination of tranquilizing medications and feeding her snacks whenever her panic and stress condition erupted.

I was extremely successful in this exercise, but it did have its consequences. I finally ended up filling my jacket pockets with Weka's snacks so they would be within easy reach. The smell of the snacks was so intense that it even overwhelmed my aftershave and my classic men's perfume. I simply smelled like dog food wherever I went! I had the feeling that was the only way people identified my presence at any location.

As soon as the underground train, tram, or the bus began pulling into the station, or the door of the lift opened, I would put a snack into Weka's mouth, and she would immediately forgot her psychic condition. There would be peace. But I could not sustain this activity for much longer, as it placed an extra burden on me, and, at the moment, my office work was highly demanding.

When Weka was not in harness in her free time, she enthusiastically enjoyed swimming, deep water diving, and rolling in the grass. She was especially skilful in sniffing out stream water deposits. When she located one, she disappeared like a spirit into it for a deep dive. One evening after work, I let her off for a walk in the grass in front of Gate One. She disappeared into the bushes and rolled in the grass for an unusually long time before we could proceed to the underground train station.

Inside the underground train, people avoided my guide

dog and me, and our section soon became empty. What a strange situation! I then noticed that my guide dog was the cause of people fleeing from us. Weka was stinking unbearably, and the smell filled our entire section of the train. She had been rolling in another dog's mess and smearing it all over her body before we entered the train. The other passengers behaved the same way when we changed to the bus at the Landstrasse still on our home journey.

When we reached our home, we could not enter the flat because of Weka's horrible, strong smell. I informed Renate about our ordeal, and she felt so sorry for me. She snapped Weka into her harness and walked her straight to the Wiener Prater, a nearby recreational landscape in our district. With no special ceremonies, Weka swiftly disappeared into the Heustadlwasser, a popular clean stream, and had a good swim, in which she included several thorough deep-water dives. When they returned to the flat, Weka had been meticulously washed and was no longer a stinking dog.

The therapy prescribed by the veterinary surgeon and domestic animal psychologist did not help to remedy Weka's condition. In fact, she got even worse with the constant intake of medications. I was happy when the trainer in Germany informed me that a replacement for her was ready. In July 1987, I travelled to the school in Germany to return Weka and collect my new guide dog. The trainer introduced me to Eiko, a shorthair German shepherd dog. As I was, by now, an old hand with dogs, we quickly made friends, and I trained with him at the school for a week. Like all the other dogs, Eiko was a very intelligent and lovable canine.

I hastily returned with Eiko to Vienna to continue my work in the office on the mid point review of the implementation of the World Programme of Action. At home, Eiko was a true family member, and, on the road and at work, he was a professional guide. My life was now back to normal, and I could mingle with people freely anywhere. Eiko was a precisionist when he was on duty. He noticed every tiny object, like needles, buttons, and sheets of paper on the floor. He steered me safely around them without letting me step on them. Once on the lift in an underground train station, a little boy said to his mother, 'Look, Mum, the dog has eyes!' The four-year-old boy had noticed the way Eiko's eyes moved and focused on his mother's finger as she pushed the right button for the floor she wanted.

I was informed a few months later by the trainer that Weka had gone to live and work with a young blind fellow in Oxburg, a little village in Germany. She was doing very well there and, unlike in Vienna, was not showing any negative or strange mental condition. I was happy to hear about Weka's normalized mental working condition. But this certainly confirmed the opinion I had maintained all along that Weka was more of a country girl than a city girl.

In August 1987 in Stockholm, the government of Sweden hosted and, jointly with our office, financed the Global Meeting of Experts to Review the Implementation of the World Programme of Action at the Mid-point of the Decade of Disabled Persons. The participants included twenty-three experts selected in their individual capacities and on the basis of equitable geographical distribution. Among the experts were fifteen persons with disabilities. Representatives of the specialized agencies of the UN system and non-governmental organizations working in the field of disability also attended the meeting.

It was the first meeting organized by the UN that would employ the use of sign language interpretation, as well as documentation in Braille and audio cassette formats, which were made possible through the financial support of the Voluntary Fund for the Decade of Disabled Persons and other external sources. I had the overall responsibility of coordinating the production of the documents of the meeting in accessible formats to disabled participants. It was a formidable task. The World Programme of Action was only published in English Braille, but it must be accessible in all the six official languages of the UN (English, French, Spanish, Arabic, Russian, and Chinese). I negotiated with the chief of the interpretation unit of the Conference Services in Vienna to use their interpreters for producing audio recordings of the documents.

I laboured painstakingly with the conference services in Vienna and the Swedish Organization of the Handicapped in Stockholm to produce the documents for the meeting in accessible formats. A good many staff members of the interpretation unit of Conference Services in Vienna volunteered to read the documents onto an audio recording machine. These professionals delivered exceptionally good quality readings in the individual official languages of the UN. I further negotiated with the electronics workshop to have the master tapes of these recordings duplicated. The recordings were then distributed to the recipients in advance of the meeting. The Swedish Organization of the Handicapped transcribed into Braille the other pre-session documents, such as the Draft Work Programme and the analysis report of the monitoring questionnaire.

Throughout the one-week duration of the meeting, our office was practically moved with its entire professional staff to the conference centre in Hasseluden, Stockholm. The director-general of the UN office in Vienna led our working team on the mission. Only a handful of the secretarial staff of the disabled persons unit was left behind to cover temporarily essential services in our office. We were joined in Stockholm by the relevant staff from the conference services in Vienna and the executive office in New York. In keeping with UN practice, we flew on different aeroplanes to Stockholm, so that if the unexpected happened, there would be staff of the organization available to accomplish the mission underway.

We arrived at the Stockholm International Airport and were driven straight to the conference centre in Hasseluden. After obligatory routine registration at reception, I was escorted to my room, where I immediately applied my typhlonautic skills to explore and identify the facilities in my new environment. I was impressed by the logical layout of the objects. I could navigate easily in the room and utilize the facilities. After settling down comfortably in the room, I found on my reading table a folder with a descriptive map of the entire conference centre and its facilities in Braille. This was an immense boost to my independence and mobility. I could easily navigate from my room to the meeting areas, the restaurant, and other rooms without assistance. Our Swedish hosts fairly understood what 'equalization of opportunities' means to a disabled person.

As our work began in earnest, I coordinated with the Swedish Organization of the Blind to produce the in-session documents of the meeting in Braille. As the documents became available in print, they were transcribed into Braille at the organization's facility in Stockholm and brought to the conference centre in Hasseluden in time to be distributed to the visually impaired participants. Thanks to our sustained hard work and proper coordination, the visually impaired participants could read the in-session documents immediately so they could contribute to the discussions on equal footing with others. This service was highly appreciated by everyone, which made us feel really proud for the success.

In their deliberations based on the report of the monitoring questionnaire, the experts considered progress made and obstacles encountered in the implementation of the World Programme of Action during the first half of the decade. They recommended a series of measures for the remaining five years to be undertaken at the regional, national, and international levels. The thirty recommendations made by the experts reflected the determination of the international community to overcome the initial difficulties of the first five years of the decade and to accomplish far greater success during the second half.

We returned from the global meeting of experts in Stockholm to Vienna with a mighty bottle that was virtually half full. I was particularly moved at the knowledge that success was identifiable in some areas of our work. But, in other areas, success was lacking because of inadequate financial resources. The UN disability programme was, by default, seriously affected by the financial constraints in the entire Secretariat in the middle of the 1980s due to the restructuring process, especially in the social and economic sector.

It was a great relief to see a group of Scandinavian countries stepping in to support the UN disability programme at a very crucial moment in its history. I cherished the generous voluntary financial contributions of these countries to the UN in my area of responsibility. The governments of Sweden, Finland, and Norway provided extra-budgetary monies and staff to strengthen our office, especially for research studies and publications in the field of disability. The contributions of the Norwegian government in this regard made it possible to prepare and publish the 'Manual of Equalization of Opportunities for Disabled Persons'. To promote proper use of the manual, the Swedish government financed the development of the 'Guidelines for Workshops on Equalization of Opportunities for Disabled Persons'.

Surely, it was not a coincidence that the notion of equalization of opportunities for disabled persons originated in Scandinavia. The secretary-general was able to appoint his special representative for the promotion of the UN

Decade of Disabled Persons through special voluntary financial contributions from concerned sources, especially the Scandinavian countries. The special representative, a Norwegian national, brought with him a wide range of experience and knowledge, which generated greater impetus for the Decade. I enjoyed working closely with him, as his office was attached to the CSDHA in Vienna.

By now, I was privileged, as a staff member and an insider, to witness the full commitment of the UN to the new trend in the civil rights movement of disabled persons, which emerged with IYDP and became vociferous during the Decade. The movement had a powerful effect on the UN and the international community. It was a major contribution, which changed the way persons with disabilities were viewed by society. Disabled persons were now considered first and foremost as citizens with equal rights and not simply as consumers of services. Even though the stigma remained in society, the perception had been transformed through heightened awareness and persistent action.

The UN Department of Public Information implemented an awareness programme with a film production entitled *Breaking Barriers*. The film documented the achievements of individuals with disabilities in different parts of the world. I featured prominently in the film as the flagship of the UN on disability. In March 1988, the camera and recording crew of the department in New York came specifically to Vienna to document my routine activities at work, on the road, and at home. My guide dog Eiko was definitely the star. We convincingly demonstrated in the film how we commuted from my home by trains and buses to the office, and how we negotiated our way throughout the VIC complex building. The crew filmed and recorded Eiko and me for two days. When *Breaking Barriers* was finally released, it was one of the main highlights of the successful outcome of the Decade of Disabled Persons.

Renate and I had known for a while that Eiko was experiencing a very serious digestion problem. Three months following his arrival from Germany, he developed intestinal diarrhoea. Our veterinary surgeon examined Eiko and diagnosed him as having a degenerative pancreas. He suggested some dietary feeding routines, which never helped to remedy Eiko's condition in any way. I informed the trainer at the guide dog school in Germany, anxious about the long time it would take him to replace Eiko.

It was a very stressful and complicated period for my dog and me since my office was located on the thirteenth floor. Eiko was a very clever dog, and he could figure out ways to help himself. But often, when he signalled to be taken outdoors to the lawn, we did not have time to organize the lift to exit the building. Each time an accident happened in our office room, the cleaning ladies were exceptionally helpful during our embarrassing and uncomfortable situation.

At the invitation of the trainer, I travelled in August 1988 to Germany to return Eiko to the school for another guide dog. When I arrived at the school, I was introduced to Pitt, a big, shorthair German shepherd. He was mainly black in colour, good looking, serene, and very intelligent. He had a fierce look in his face as if he had poked his head into and out of a chimney hole. After the initial caresses and nuzzles, we quickly became friends. I trained with him at the school for another week before returning to Vienna with him. Renate, Esther, and Jacqueline came to the railway station to welcome us. They were very impressed by our new family friend, whom they wished would not have to be returned again so soon to the school in Germany.

After a couple of days, my wife and the children went back to Puchberg on the Schneeberg (mountain), where we had rented a family house for our summer holidays. During the week, Pitt and I stayed in Vienna and went to work. On weekends, I travelled by train from Vienna to join my family.

Puchberg is a popular resort town in the south of Vienna. One of its most famous tourist attractions is the cogwheel train which transports tourists to the top of the Schneeberg. One weekend, I went with my family to have dinner in one of the hotels in the town. I was immensely amused when my wife read the dessert section of the menu to me, which said, 'Moor in a Shirt, a special recommendation by the chef'. When the chef came to our table, I stood up and said to him cheerfully, 'Thank you, chef, for honouring my visit to your hotel with moor in a shirt.' He thought briefly, and then bust into loud laughter. Everyone in the dining hall of the hotel also laughed. Smiling broadly, the chef said to me, 'Sir, I invite you and your family to a complimentary treat—our special moor in a shirt.' It was a delicious black chocolate dessert, which my family and I greatly enjoyed.

I wanted to live a life style that reminded me of my childhood village environment, but I didn't want to diminish the level of my present standard of living. I had lived in Vienna since my arrival in Austria. The city had given me almost everything I needed to support a comfortable level of well-being, especially family, education, and employment. I was married to a young lady of the city, Renate Schneider, and we had two daughters—Esther and Jacqueline.

But deciding to try to strike a balance between living in the countryside and working in the city was not an easy choice to make. In 1989, I resolved to build a family house on a sizeable plot of land, which I had purchased in 1985 in Eichgraben, a little village in the west of Vienna. It was a beautiful piece of land in the Viennese Wood. Half of the estate was woodland with a lot of big oak trees, and the other half was grassland. We built our family house right in the centre between the two equal parts of the estate.

Our ultimate preference for living in the countryside was only made possible by the significant improvement in train services between the west of the city of Vienna and the its surrounding villages in the 1980s. It took me about sixty minutes for the forty-kilometre journey from my home in Eichgraben to my office at the Vienna International Centre. Trains were available every hour or half an hour to the main stations in the west of Vienna, either at Hütteldorf or Westbahnhof. Renate usually drove us to and picked us up from the railway station in Eichgraben. When she could not do so, we swiftly walked the fifteen-minute route on our own.

Pitt was quick to master our new itinerary. I had two alternative choices to go by train from our home in Eichgraben to my workplace. In Hütteldorf, I took the underground train and changed to another one, either at Karlsplatz or Schwedenplatz to the Vienna International Centre. Or, at Westbahnhof, I took the underground train and changed to another one at Stephansplatz.

It was a very convenient commuter service. I could comfortably sit on the train, relax, have a little nap, read Braille magazines, or prepare drafts of documents for the office. At the end of our daily journeys, when I stepped out of the train in Eichgraben, I would notice that all the accumulated stresses from the office had dissipated.

Our decision to acquire our own landed property and build our own family house in the countryside was like catching two birds with one stone. On one hand, we enjoyed fully all the necessities that nature could afford. On the other, I successfully pursued my professional career in the city. My daughters regularly mailed greeting cards to their friends with the inscription 'Many greetings to you from our living and holiday location, Eichgraben'.

I remember clearly the day we finally moved out of our flat in Vienna. Our belongings, including over 180 cartons, each labelled with a description of its contents, were loaded onto a big lorry for our exodus. I stood on the pavement in front of Hagenmüllergasse 23 in the 3rd district and wondered how much the people were going to miss their 'favourite little black man of the district and his dapper guide dog'.

We moved into our new home in Eichgraben on a snowy winter day in December 1989. It was a very happy occasion, which my family and I celebrated joyously. Our joy was electrified by the memorable events that were taking place on the Austrian borders at the same time. Since November 1989, the Berlin Wall—the Iron Curtain, the symbol of the cold war—had begun to fall unabatedly.

As we settled down in our new home, we listened over the radio and watched on television as the celebrations and the joy of the people unfolded. East Germans and West Germans, who had been the forefront victims of the cold war, were being reunited. These events progressed rapidly in the following months, eventually leading to the collapse of the Soviet Union in 1991.

The liberalisms brought about by the policy of glasnost (openness and transparency of government and freedom of information) and perestroika (restructuring and reorganization of society), introduced in the Soviet Union in the second half of the 1980s, coupled with the sustained efforts of the Western powers for peaceful coexistence in Europe and the rest of the world, had contributed to the end of the cold war, which had endured from 1947 to 1991. The cold war had been the continuing state of political conflict, military tension, proxy wars, and economic competition that existed between Eastern and Western powers after the Second World War.

Pitt enthusiastically loved our new natural environment in the countryside. When he was not on duty, I would take him out for walks of many hours in any weather condition in the wood surrounding our neighbourhood, which was free of cars and city road traffic. But I was constantly reminded of my childhood experience whenever I walked into the wood and breathed deeply in and out saying, 'How beautiful is nature'. Once, as a child, as I stood admiring nature, I also stood with my full weight on a poor little ant that had laboured all day long gathering her food and materials for building her pyramid. I looked under my foot and wondered if nature was also beautiful for the poor little innocent ant, which was now dead. I recognized that nature was absolutely beautiful for us to admire, as she was the whole of all creatures. Every creature—human or otherwise—was ultimately subjected to destiny.

As well as the big trees in the forest, I particularly enjoyed the free entertainment provided by the thousands of birds around us in all seasons of the year. Every summer, these naturally gifted birds began singing their beautiful songs as early as half past three in the morning. I definitely preferred to be awakened by these songs rather than by the noises of cars in the city. These songs were my indispensable alarm clock, since I woke up every workday at four o'clock to prepare for work.

Every day, I would take my dog out for an early morning work, and meticulously groom him for the day. After having breakfast and a shower, I would dress in time to catch the seven o'clock train to Vienna. This ensured that I was in my office before eight o'clock at the Vienna International Centre.

I clearly understood that the compound of our landed property must be properly maintained in all weather and at all times. In winter, depending on the intensity of the snowfall, I frequently cleared the snow which had fallen along the forty-metre path from our house entrance to the gate on the main street and the eighty-square-metre area in front of our house and the terrace. In summer, I swept the same areas to get rid of the millions of dry leaves which had fallen from the oak trees. I regularly performed these tasks in darkness, either in the morning or in the evening, mostly to the astonishment of my sighted neighbours. I passionately enjoyed doing so because it was the only time I could take judicious revenge with my sighted neighbours, since they could not effectively compete with me in performing similar activities around their homes in darkness.

Living in Eichgraben was a genuine source of happiness and self-fulfilment for me. One evening, Pitt and I arrived late from the office by train at the station in Eichgraben. Renate was not at hand to pick us up from the railway station, so we began walking home down the hill from the station to the main road. I noticed that a gentleman walking ahead of us had stopped to greet me. He introduced himself to me as the mayor of our village. As we walked together down the hill chatting, he told me that he was going for a 'cling of the glass' with the firefighters of our village because the captain was celebrating his birthday.

Then, the mayor suddenly asked me in a very friendly voice, "'Doctor, tell me, what has made you come to live with us in Eichgraben?' I was highly amused by his question. I replied, 'Oh, mayor, do you know what? As I lived in Vienna for many years, I always heard that only the nobler citizens lived in Eichgraben. So I decided to join them.' The mayor burst into such a loud laughter that the echo of his voice filled the empty space of the viaduct under which we were passing at the moment. I also laughed very loud, and we had a lot of fun until we parted from each other that evening.

At home and at work, I was torn between settling down in our new home and preparing for another major international event. Thanks to the generous technical and financial contribution by the government of Finland, another Scandinavian country, our office organized the International Experts Group Meeting on Alternative Ways to Mark the End of the Decade of Disabled Persons in 1992. The meeting was hosted by the Finnish government, and was held from 7 to 11 May 1990 in Helsinki.

I travelled with my colleagues to Helsinki to service the experts meeting in collaboration with our Finnish hosts. As at other events, my main task was to facilitate the participation of the disabled experts in terms of providing them access to the physical environment and documentation of the meeting. Our Finnish hosts were extremely equal to the task. They understood the practical needs of disabled persons. The physical environment of the meeting was friendly and barrier free. We coordinated our efforts to provide all the documentation in accessible formats.

Our office was gratified by the generosity of the Finnish government in financing the meeting. It was a most welcome rescue operation for the disability programme. The experts advised our office on our preparation of a feasibility study on the substantive, financial, and administrative implications of alternative ways to mark the end of the Decade. They suggested an agenda for action from 1990 to 1993, an outline of a long-term strategy to sustain the implementation of the World Programme of Action until the year 2000 and beyond, and proposals for institutional arrangements to facilitate implementation of the principal recommendations in the agenda for action.

Given the prevailing chronic financial constraints of the

UN, not all the recommendations of the experts could be implemented as desired. But our office insisted that a high-level ministerial global conference would represent a logical sequence of the events, which had begun in 1981 with the International Year of Disabled Persons.

Since no government volunteered to host and co-finance such an event, a high-level ministerial conference was held at the UN Headquarters in New York in conjunction with the annual session of the General Assembly. All governments of member states, as well as the relevant non-governmental organizations in consultative status with the Economic and Social Council, were invited to the conference.

In February 1989, an American non-governmental organization donated a Thiel Braille printer to our office for the production of grade one and grade two English Braille. This ability to produce documents in Braille internally was a real boost for our office. It substantially strengthened my professional profile, as I was the only staff member with the required skills to operate and supervise the Braille production.

With my promotion to a higher professional grade, the number of duties assigned to me increased substantially. They included, among other things, organizing the inter-agency meeting, coordinating inter-agency affairs and the project on the international information network, producing Braille information materials, contributing to the UN yearbooks of 1989, 1990, and 1991 on the disability programme, carrying out administrative work, and writing routine correspondence.

In organizing the annual inter-agency meeting, I coordinated all relevant administrative and technical arrangements and prepared the final reports. Essentially, the purpose of the inter-agency meeting was to serve as a forum for consultations on programmes coordination of the activities of the UN system in the field of disability. These consultations were especially instrumental in the formulation of the World Programme of Action during the 1981 International Year of Disabled Persons.

The unwavering support of my guide dog was indispensable in my ability to organize these inter-agency meetings effectively. As the substantive professional staff member responsible, I had specific logistical, administrative, and technical tasks to carry out before, during, and after the meetings. Pitt and I rocketed on six legs like a space ship between the various sections of the building, offices, and conference rooms and through the corridors to follow up on correspondences to overcome last minute surprises.

Before each inter-agency meeting, I prepared the annotated agenda on which to guide the discussions, information notes to the participants on formalities and facilities available, and the programme of work and time schedules on the various agenda items. I wrote the opening statement of the director-general, or a designated staff member. Finally, I produced these documents in Braille using the Thiel Braille printer to facilitate the participation of the visually impaired at the meeting. As the secretary, I sat on the podium along with the head of our office, who chaired the meeting. I recorded the minutes of the discussions, highlighting the salient points and writing up the final report.

However, finalizing the report and transcribing it into Braille for adoption by the participants the following morning was a highly tricky and stressful affair. On one occasion, I stayed in the office until the early morning hours to finish the report when all the trains had stopped running and I could not catch one to take Pitt and me home. On another occasion, I spent a few hours in the VIC staff rest room and took the early morning trains at four o'clock to Eichgraben. Arriving home at seven o'clock, I quickly walked my dog, took breakfast, had a shower, and dressed. Renate drove us to the railway station to catch the eight o'clock train back to Vienna. The concluding session of the inter-agency meeting resumed on time at ten o'clock. I was greatly relieved that the final report was ready, both in print and Braille, for adoption by the participants.

As the UN Decade of Disabled Persons was rapidly coming to a close, our office was invited to attend the third International Abilympics in Hong Kong from 10 to 14 August 1991. I was automatically designated to accompany the director of our social development division to the event. My experience was indispensable in making the necessary preparations for the journey, as I had participated in the first International Abilympics ten years earlier in Tokyo in 1981. I wrote the message of the secretary-general to the participants, the textual intervention of our office to the panel discussions, as well as information notes on our activities, which were transmitted to newspaper agencies in Hong Kong for publication prior to the event.

Having rigorously completed the preparations for our journey, I flew with the director from Vienna to Hong Kong via the Frankfurt International Airport. On arrival in Hong Kong, a delegation of the organizing committee was at hand to welcome us, along with other participants who arrived at the same time. Two young lady students quickly introduced themselves to me as my volunteer assistants throughout the duration of the International Abilympics. They accompanied me in the car to my hotel accommodation in the city and assisted me with the registration procedures at the reception desk.

As my guides ushered me into my hotel room, I immediately conjured my typhlonautic skills to explore the new environment. I identified all the facilities and orientation cues to enable my flawless and 'normal' movement in the room. I familiarized myself with the location of the bathroom and its appliances, and then the bedroom—furniture, gadgets and equipment, the window and the blinds, electric switches and sockets, and the door to the corridor. Finally, I settled down to unpack the contents of my suitcase. Before I left home, Renate, as always, had supported me in arranging and labelling in Braille my clothing and other items in the suitcase. I was confident that I would be colour coordinated for every anticipated occasion during the event.

Over 2000 participants from eighty-three countries competed in the third International Abilympics in Hong Kong and its accompanying events. I sat with the audience in the stadium at the opening of the event and proudly listened as our director delivered the message of the secretary-general, which I had written, to the participants. The commissioner of social security delivered the message of the U.S. president, and the high-level representation of the United States added to the splendour of the event.

Following the opening extravaganzas, it was time for us to tackle the actual business. The director and I divided the tasks of our representation between us equally—meeting the various press agencies and giving interviews, participating in the panel discussions, and visiting the different pavilions of the skills contests. The central topic of the panel discussions was on the application of new technology, training, and employment of disabled persons.

In the paper that I had prepared for the panel discussions, I addressed the UN record of accomplishment in the field of disability, the development and application of new technology for human resources development, and full integration of disabled persons into society. I explained that it was the policy of the UN to support the development and application of new technology in the disability area.

As a part of my tasks in covering the events, I gave interviews to the news media, including radio and television, on the Decade of Disabled Persons. I was exceedingly pleased that the information I provided was published in a special supplement of the *Hong Kong Economic Journal*.

Before finally leaving Hong Kong at the end of the events, the director and I warmly thanked the Royal Hong Kong Jockey Club on behalf of the UN for their contribution to the success of the third International Abilympics. Their efforts had helped to put Hong Kong on the map as one of the strongest supporters of programmes on disability in the world.

Throughout our stay in Hong Kong, the director and I followed with great interest and profound appreciation the numerous signs of the club's involvement in the organization of the Abilympics. In addition to the indefatigable efforts of over 1000 individual volunteers, the club had been the driving force to move the project ahead. It was most instrumental in providing facilities for the splendid organization of the two major events of the Abilympics: the International Conference on Development of Innovative Training and Employment for People with Disabilities, and the record-breaking contest for the longest-dancing dragon.

The director and I left Hong Kong deeply touched by the message of the third International Abilympics and the emotional experience it had given to all its participants. For most of them, some of the events must have been the highlights of their lives. In the sense of participation, they were all winners ... record breakers ... along with the longest dancing dragon, the head of which the organizers presented to the UN office at Vienna.

On our return to Vienna, we contacted the founders of an extremely interesting project for children, called SOS Children's Villages. They had several dozen villages for children and foster mothers all over Austria and in other European countries. One such village was located near Vienna. We organized with the founders of this interesting project a small ceremony in autumn 1991, during which we presented the dragon's head to the children's village near Vienna. We used the occasion to tell the audience the story of the dragon and to report on the noble ideas behind the Abilympics.

Meanwhile, advances in information technology were accelerating globally, and the UN recognized the benefit of these developments in exchanging information on disability. Following up on this recognition, I coordinated a Roundtable Consultation on the Establishment of an Information Network and Database on Disability at our office. The event was held at the Vienna International Centre, and the participants were information technology experts from the disability sections of the UN specialized agencies and relevant non-governmental organizations.

The experts recommended the development of our own internal information system. We were relieved when the Computer and Automation Institute of the Hungarian Academy of Sciences implemented, free of charge, a pilot project on a specialised database on disability in our office.

The programme budget of our office for 1990 and 1991 included an output to develop an information network for collecting and disseminating data on disability. But the resources required for the project could not be fully mobilized at once. Initially, the only financial support we received was from the voluntary fund and from generous voluntary contributions by the governments of Sweden and Finland. With this limited financial support, we engaged two young, smart experts of the Institute of Computers and Information Engineering, Warsaw, Poland, under contract, to develop the prototype software for the database.

I had only one general staff member assigned to support me in the day-to-day work on the database. Once the information was recorded, we utilized the database to identify documents, institutions, activities, and projects on specific aspects of disability in different countries and regions. We obtained detailed information on documents or projects of an institution, maintained up-to-date knowledge on documents that were on loan, and prepared mailing lists according to the various criteria.

As resources became modestly available, we employed a young computer specialist to help carry forward the implementation of the prototype software for the database on a microcomputer. I proposed to call our database 'CLEAR', and my proposal was readily accepted. Given our high expectations of CLEAR, we were motivated to announce its establishment and further development to the relevant offices of the UN system and non-governmental organizations.

In a beautifully designed leaflet, we highlighted the long-time pressing need to establish a worldwide system for the collection and dissemination of disability-related information to enhance the coordination of activities in this field. I coordinated the workshop, organized by our office at the Vienna International Centre, on 5 and 6 October 1992, to present the structure and functions of CLEAR formally, and to solicit collaboration from other offices of the UN system and non-governmental organizations.

As we were wholly dependent on the availability of extra-budgetary resources for the further development of CLEAR capacities, we boldly proposed in 1993 our cooperation with the International Disability Foundation in Geneva, given its special focus on non-governmental organizations concerned with disability issues. The cooperation took the form of provision of software developed especially for the UN to support the CLEAR project and the secondment of a project research officer through the financial contribution by the government of Italy. But the implementation of the project was rescheduled due to recruitment delays.

In 1993, the Centre for Social Development and Humanitarian Affairs, along with the UN Disability Programme moved from Vienna, back to the UN Headquarters in New York. The move required that professional staff on regular posts who had been international recruits must be transferred to the new duty station.

The general staff, such as the secretarial and manual staff, and professionals on extra-budgetary posts, were not affected by the move. As they were not international, but local, recruits, they could not be transferred with their posts to New York. Their employment with the UN was automatically terminated. But the UNOV Administration and the UNOV Staff Council made strenuous efforts to help every affected staff member to be absorbed by other UN offices and programmes in Vienna.

For personal and family reasons, I opted to stay behind in Vienna, even though I was sitting on a regular professional post and had been internationally recruited. I was fully aware of the administrative implications of my decision—that I would be abandoned behind in Vienna without a job if I did not go onboard the ship for the journey to the new duty station. It was a period of tremendous anxiety for me as I relied totally on the efforts and goodwill of the UNOV administration and the UNOV staff council for help. I wrote a personal interoffice memorandum to the director of UNOV administration on the matter accordingly.

Administration eventually succeeded in identifying a suitable post and an office to retain me in Vienna. But, before the necessary administrative arrangements could be finalized for my deployment, I continued to work on some activities of the disability programme directly from Vienna. Most of the tasks I accomplished in this manner were local activities that were left behind by the rest of the team before the move to New York. This state of affair lasted until the end of 1993.

At the beginning of 1994, I joined the UN Information Service in Vienna (UNIS-Vienna) as information officer. I settled down quickly in my new job, despite the new style of working. The tasks were frequently marked 'rush!' instead of 'urgent!' as I was used to in my former office. Now there were new levels of importance and speed required in carrying out assignments.

But I found the job personally fulfilling. I researched and analyzed information materials, writing up the *UN Weekly* (a summary news on UN system-wide activities). As well as writing press releases of meetings, conferences, seminars and workshops, I researched and translated German newspaper articles on UN-related issues, and prepared daily summary reports, which were transmitted to headquarters in New York for issuance. Part of my public relations duties also included giving regular lectures to visitors at the Vienna International Centre on UN history, programmes, and activities worldwide.

Advances in access technology had by now improved significantly, and brought about significant enhancement in my method of work in the office. Dolphin Computer Access Limited had developed software called Hal for blind computer users. Designed for use at home, at work, and in education, Hal could read the computer screen interactively and communicate the text through a speech synthesiser or a refreshable Braille display.

Telesensory Systems Incorporated had developed OpenBook, an optical character recognition technology which offered blind and visually impaired computer users the ability to scan printed text and then hear it spoken back in synthetic speech or saved to a computer.

With the acquisition of Hal and OpenBook, and their installation on my personal computer in combination with the refreshable Braille display, my workstation was now sufficiently equipped to help me meet the challenges of my new office. Added to that, I received office automation training on electronic mail application software and access to the Local Area Network system within the entire working environment at UNOV.

With these technologies now fully at my disposal, I scanned and browsed through the numerous German-language newspapers, which our information desk clerk had collected for me. I extracted the relevant articles on UN policies appearing in these newspapers and stored them in my computer. I then edited and translated them into English for transmission to Headquarters in New York.

This task was the first thing I usually did every morning when I arrived in my office. I made sure that the texts were finalized and transmitted promptly to headquarters by three in the afternoon Vienna time, so that the materials were included in the daily press briefings by the spokesman's office of the secretary-general at noon each day in New York.

Writing press releases on the meetings of intergovernmental bodies held in Vienna was another glaring challenge that I skilfully managed with the application of my adaptive technologies. When these meetings were in session, the individual UN Information Service (UNIS) professional staff members who were assigned to cover the meeting sat in the conference room to monitor and take notes on the proceedings. The notes had to be edited, compiled, and finalized before they could be included in press releases. For most meetings, four professionals were assigned to cover the proceedings.

The conference rooms for the major meetings were located in the huge building complex of the VIC, far away from the location of UNIS offices. I could not move my office equipment to the conference room area without encountering immense complications and hardship. So I stayed in my office to accomplish any task related to meeting coverage.

A remote listening device, nicknamed 'squawk', was installed in some UNIS offices, including mine. It consisted of a little box that contained a loudspeaker and was mounted on the wall, and it was connected through cabling to the interpreters' booth in the conference room. Another option for me was to dial in to the interpreters' booth with a designated telephone number, and then use the loudspeaker of the telephone on my desk. Applying these optional techniques meant I sat comfortably at my office desk and listened to the proceedings of the meetings as if I were actually physically present in the conference room.

The meetings were divided into morning and afternoon sessions. The morning sessions usually went from ten to one, and the afternoon sessions from three to six. In writing the press releases, we shared the tasks amongst ourselves as a team. Two professional colleagues took notes from the conference, room and I took notes from my office through a loudspeaker. A third professional colleague sat in her office and collated on her computer the texts we had passed on to her through the LAN network system.

As a team, we utilized to the fullest the office automation and the local network computer system at UNOV to accomplish the tasks. We shared the tasks equitably amongst ourselves, taking turns to write up the relevant and salient issues highlighted by the individual speakers in their intervention on the conference floor in the meeting room. Colleague A took notes whilst the first speaker was speaking, and colleague B took notes on the second speaker. I took on the third speaker. Before it got to my turn again to take on the sixth speaker, I would have written up my contribution on the intervention of the third speaker and passed the text on to colleague C through the computer access local network system to collate for the press release. It was a very stressful operation.

Taking full advantage of the time difference between Vienna and New York, we made sure that the press releases on the morning session of the meetings were ready and transmitted to headquarters before offices opened there. We applied similar procedure for the press releases for the afternoon session of the meetings, making sure that the press releases were ready and transmitted to headquarters at the end of their lunch break.

My deployment as information officer with UNIS Vienna could not have happened at a more auspicious moment in my career with the UN. In 1995, numerous events and activities were organized at the local, national, and international levels to celebrate the fiftieth anniversary of the creation of the UN. As an international civil servant, I felt extremely privileged to be part of this unique moment in the history of the organization.

As a consequence of this celebration, an unprecedented number of groups of visitors poured in daily to the Vienna International Centre to learn about the UN. When giving special briefings and lectures to these groups of visitors at the VIC, as they would have finished their guided tour of the building to listen to me, I informed them in depth about the UN and the work of the Vienna-based organizations in the fields of drugs and crime, the peaceful uses of outer space, industrial trade law, refugees, specialized agencies on industrial development, the peaceful uses of nuclear energy, and the banning of nuclear weapon testing.

I always talked enthusiastically about the origins of the UN and its underlying structures, policies, and activities. I especially enjoyed answering questions on the UN charter, written by representatives of fifty governments that met at the UN conference on international organizations, held in San Francisco, from 25 April to 26 June 1945. The governments of these member states adopted and signed this landmark document for peace in human development in modern times following the devastations of the Second World War.

I would then familiarize my audience with the six main bodies of the UN, and diligently describe the General Assembly and its seven standing committees, the Economic and Social Council and its coordination of the work of the entire UN family, including the specialized agencies, the Security Council and the issue of veto right, the Trusteeship Council and the issue of decolonization, the International Court of Justice and the election of the judges, the Secretariat and its world-wide staff and the secretary-general as the chief administrator.

I would seize the opportunity at any briefing or lecture to inform the general public about UN peacekeeping operations globally. I preferred to use examples to enumerate the various kinds of UN peacekeeping operations. The six kinds of peacekeeping operation as of the time were on preventive deployment as in the former Yugoslav Republic of Macedonia; traditional peacekeeping as in the Golan Heights or Cyprus; implementation of a comprehensive settlement as in Cambodia; secured humanitarian assistance as in Bosnia-Hezegovina; restoration of states' sovereignty as in Somalia or Rwanda; peace enforcement under Chapter VII of the UN charter as in the 1991 Gulf Crisis. My listeners generally appreciated this approach, which always made me a proud international civil servant.

Now, old age and chronic illness were rapidly taking toll of my poor guide dog, Pitt. When I had first fetched him from the guide dog school in Germany at the age of three to begin working with me, he was a little older than the average guide dog. We had barely worked together for three months when the veterinary doctor diagnosed him with degenerative pancreas, an illness similar to the one that had affected my previous dog Eiko. But this time around, our new veterinary doctor was very clever, indeed. He prescribed a life-long canine diet for Pitt that helped to keep the illness under control.

But the chronic spinal pains, which Pitt had fought off so successfully for several years, could no longer be controlled with therapeutic intervention. The veterinary doctor finally pronounced him unable to work and sent him on early certified retirement at nine years of age rather than at ten years, which was the normal retirement age for a guide dog.

I did not have to wait for a replacement guide dog at all. Before Pitt went on retirement, I fetched another guide dog from Hungary. He was a very young long-haired German shepherd. At the age of seventeen months he was highly intelligent. His name was Nico, and I also called him Nicky. He was extremely friendly and playful, but he knew no compromise when in business and in harness. A twenty-five-year-old young lady had trained Nico, and female folks of that age group always attracted him.

Pitt gladly welcomed Nico to our home. They had a very cordially relationship—almost like that of a father and his son. But Pitt always looked sad whenever he had to stay behind at home and watch Nico get dressed up in harness for work. They played happily together when we returned from work and at the weekends. I also enjoyed having a guide dog on retirement and another one in active service. Whatever Nico might have missed learning at the guide dog school, he quickly and comfortably picked up from the 'daddy dog' at home. What a compensation, indeed!

Like his predecessors, Nico was exceptionally intelligent. He very quickly mastered our route to the office from our home in Eichgraben. When we arrived in Vienna by the suburban train, we continued our daily journey from Hütteldorf with the underground train to the station Schwedenplatz. There, we took a lift to the next floor, then turned right and walked about fifteen steps to another lift, which brought us down to the level of another underground train.

One morning, we got out of the first lift, turned right and walked a few steps towards the next lift. We were only a few metres away from the lift when Nico abruptly stopped and became thoughtful for a moment. Then he turned round and walked hastily in the opposite direction until we arrived at another lift about fifty metres away that also took us down to the U1 underground station.

As we waited for the lift to arrive, a lady, who had run to catch up with us, asked me in a gentle voice, 'Can your guide dog read?' I asked, 'Why?' She said, 'A signboard is placed in front of the second lift over there saying it is out of order and that travellers are advised to take the lift on the exit to Rotenturmstrasse.' I told her that my dog could not read, but that we had found ourselves in a similar situation some months ago when someone had helped us out of the dilemma. My guide dog remembered exactly that scenario and had taken the appropriate corrective action without my intervention.

This incredible but routine performance of my guide dog was even reported in one of the Austrian national newspapers. Nico had become so popular in and outside the

Vienna International Centre that many staff members were asking me too many questions about my longhaired German shepherd dog. To take care of these questions in an amusing manner, I wrote the following article, which was published in the UNOV Staff Journal:

Do you remember me? Well, if not, let me then formally introduce myself to you. I'm the gentleman who is always accompanied by a woollen, four-legged friend. Perhaps, you may have seen us around in the building. Don't worry if you can't remember right away. You're not alone in this situation. Folks don't see me first. They usually see my four-legged friend because he is always ahead of me, and I squat and walk very obediently behind him. Do you now remember me? Eh, thank goodness it's so easy to let you know!

Now, having introduced myself to you, may I tell you that my friend is a very clever one. He takes me to the office and brings me back home everyday. He's a professional guide, and that's what he's been trained to do. As I said earlier, he has four legs and I've only two. We manage very well together as I've quite conveniently adjusted to a dog's trot. Do you want to walk beside us for a little conversation to the underground train station? Oh, yes. But you will have to double up because you are at a big disadvantage on two legs. It's much faster on six legs. Let's not miss the train, come on! Hey, look at us rocketing ahead!

I have succeeded in teaching my friend a couple of additional clever things. Although his mother tongue is Hungarian (and he was trained in German), he has picked up some English words and a couple of VIC-based idioms. These include such expressions as Bank Austria, Creditanstalt, post office, conference room area, commissary, cafeteria, bar, and so on. What a clever canine polyglot! Oh boy, you want to know how I can mark the floor of my destination if I'm alone with him on the lift! Yes, you are right. I've failed to teach him to do that just as I've not yet succeeded in teaching him to use the men's rooms upstairs. That's not too bad. At least I can join him every day at lunchtime to take fresh air outside the building on the lawn. Every disappointment is a blessing! Don't you agree?

One thing I must confess to you is that I'm very jealous of my woollen friend. Wherever we go together on our daily journeys, all the beautiful ladies and handsome gentlemen are attracted to him. They caress his soft and fluffy fur and whisper nice and soothing words into his ears while I stand by and look on. I'm totally ignored. If I complain, the ladies say, 'Ah, your friend is not as dangerous as you are!' 'He's so beautiful.' Am I then the ugly one? Never mind, that's the way of life. One thing I promise my friend is that, one day, I will resolve to walk also on four legs so I can compete effectively with him on equal footing. I bet he will still win the race as he always does!

My friend is very sociable. He loves to make new friends and to keep the old ones. So, join our band of friends when next you happen to see us in one of our scouting journeys in the building. I know you have much respect for him. Don't be afraid, he won't bite. He is a convinced vegetarian and detests meat, especially human. He won't mind if you can join him one day for a delicious vegetarian lunch in the cafeteria. How about that! *Bon appétit!*

My friend is also a very dedicated staff member and has an excellent sense of duty and responsibility. His office is well equipped with all the necessities of a modern workplace, even though he prefers to lie under his office desk. We both share a common office space. Should you telephone or pass by our office, don't hesitate to leave a message if I'm not around. In any event, my friend will receive and deliver the message to me in the appropriate format. Funny funky snap shots, aren't they?

Following the publication of that beautiful article in the *UNOV Staff Journal*, I observed that many of my colleagues who joined me at my table in the cafeteria for lunch curiously asked if my guide dog was indeed vegetarian. I answered them that I was actually the vegetarian one of us two, because I also detested human flesh just like my woollen friend. But as to the question of whether I had always been vegetarian, I swiftly responded in the negative. The relationship with my canine friends had prompted me first and foremost to give up cannibalism for vegetarianism. I was no longer willing to accept the superficial distinction between other animal meat and that of my canine friends, who had so much dedication, love and compassion for me. I thought it would be cynical, or even schizophrenic, of me, on one hand, to have pets at home and advocate for animal's rights, and yet on the other hand, to eat fish and the meat of slaughtered animals, no matter in whatever form, with cupidity. I successfully maintained my moral stance in this matter, thanks to the unwavering support of my wife and my daughters, who had themselves become convinced vegans and vegetarians long before I made my decision.

As much as I enjoyed working with UNIS Vienna, I was nevertheless thrilled when, in 1996, I transferred to the Interpretation and Meetings Section of the Division of Administration and Common Services of UNOV and was assigned to work as administrative officer for servicing conferences in Vienna. It was the climax of my ambition as a visually impaired staff member to be mainstreamed in the work environment of the UN. The work of servicing conferences in Vienna was carried out at two levels: the Translation Section and the Interpretation and Meetings Section. However, I had little or no role to play in the activities of the former.

As the administrative officer, I was assigned to the office of the chief, Interpretation and Meetings Section, which was responsible for the overall administration and management of conference servicing activities to the International Atomic Energy Agency (IAEA), United Nations Industrial Development Organization UNIDO, and the United Nations Office at Vienna within the framework of common services arrangements at the Vienna International Centre (VIC).

The office organized, coordinated, directed, reviewed, and evaluated the performance of the Interpretation Unit and the Meetings Planning, Coordination and Servicing Unit, which included Documents Reproduction, Distribution, and Correspondence. The office of the chief was comprised of two professional posts (the chief and the administrative officer) and one general service post.

My main tasks were to monitor the financial and staffing records of the section, to assist in the preparation of the draft biennial programme budgets and prepare bi-annual management plan forecasts, manage the section's high-speed photocopying services, monitor recommendations of the Committee on Conferences and their programme implications, coordinate preparations of the performance appraisal system process of the section, and prepare draft UNOV administrative instruction on the use of the VIC premises for meetings, conferences, special events, and exhibits.

These tasks were completely different from the ones I had previously performed at UNIS. They were extremely challenging and daunting, given the working tools that were presently available to me in the office. My routine work involved retrieving and reading documents and then presenting the information in tabulated forms, which I performed in a totally new working environment. To make matters even more complex, the division had switched over to the Windows application for its office automation. I had to acquire the appropriate adaptive technology and the necessary training in order to work in that environment.

It took very long and arduous negotiations in several meetings with the staff of the administration before the required funds were identified in the regular budget to purchase a Braille display with eighty cells and screen reader software for Windows. The Braille display was the CombiBraille, and the screen reader was JAWS for Windows.

These devices enabled me to obtain information stored in the section's administrative databases and from the various hardcopy forms, which I scanned into my personal computer. The tabulated texts and forms were reproduced on the Braille display and were also read to me simultaneously. What a great relief!

Now, as my office was adequately equipped with these adaptive technologies, I quickly took training in the Windows 95 application and the e-mail operation in a Nouvel network environment relevant to the office automation of the division. Furnished with these skills and secretarial support, I was able to meet the challenges of my administrative duties for servicing conferences effectively.

My job to monitor and follow up on the financial and staffing records of the Interpretation and Meetings Section involved liaising regularly with the staffs of the UNOV Finance and Budget Section and the Human Resources Management Section. In that connection, I reviewed the monthly issuance of the status of account as well as the periodic allotment advice and the overtime and compensatory time-off reports of individual staff members. I checked properly for consistency with the allotted expenditure, and that the claims of staff for payment of special post allowances, overtime, and compensatory time off were duly processed.

Naturally, preparing and monitoring the implementation of the biennial programme budget of the division was an important activity of the administrative officers of all the sections. When I took on my administrative job, the implementation of the section's programme budget for the biennium 1996–1997 was already ongoing. So I focused my efforts primarily on administering and monitoring the inputs and outputs that were recommended therein for servicing conferences in Vienna.

But immediately I saw myself fully involved in the preparation of the draft programme budget submission for the biennium 1998–1999 in terms of its implications for the activities of the Interpretation and Meetings Section. I prepared myself extremely well for this task by studying and analyzing the previous programme budgets for 1994–1995 and 1996–1997.

With the knowledge I acquired from those studies, I was able to direct the staff of the Interpretation Unit and the Meetings Planning and Conference Servicing Unit of our section to complete the appropriate draft programme budget submission forms, and to prepare the draft programme budget narratives. After receiving the required contributions, I diligently compiled the draft programme budget narrative of the section and the draft vision statement of the Interpretation and Meetings Section within the framework of the medium-term plan. Of course, the preparation of the draft programme budget was always a highly cumbersome and very complicated exercise. But it was a tremendous fun for me, despite all the intrigues and manipulations involved in the process.

At the same time, I was required to identify special projects in addition to the programme budget 1996–1997, which must be implemented during the current programme budget cycle. It was a task that merited serious attention. I held discussions with the chiefs of the units and collected information I used to identify the most important special projects that had not been taken into account when the current programme budget was formulated and approved for implementation.

I then discussed the identified special projects with the chief of the section. When I received her approval, I proceeded to prepare an elaborate project document for the individual special projects. The projects were submitted to the responsible office in the division for approval.

These special projects were to enlarge the document distribution area, to acquire powerful computer equipment and software for five staff of the section, to construct a ceiling in the UN documents distribution area, to acquire additional equipment, furniture, cabling, and computer training for the staff of the Interpretation Unit, and to establish United Nations Official Documentation System (ODS) terminal retrieval service for delegates at UNOV.

I further exhibited my managerial skills when I successfully assured that the effective operation of the high-speed photocopying service of the section was continued and that new contract for the high-speed photocopying machines was arranged and implemented. Following my proposals, the Purchase and Contracts Committee decided that we should go for a competitive bidding for a contract. As the bids were received in the office in sealed envelopes from the competing companies, I evaluated each submission as objectively as I possibly could. They were then submitted to the Purchase and Contracts Committee for final selection and contract award. I definitely enjoyed this activity. It was a highly contentious exercise, both within and outside the office.

But in this other task of mine, I quickly found out that monitoring the implementation of the resolutions adopted by the General Assembly on the recommendations of the Committee on Conferences was an extremely laborious job. Throughout the period of my work with conference services in Vienna, the Committee on Conferences was occupied with ways to improve utilization of conference servicing resources.

As the administrative officer in Vienna, I played a crucial role in those activities by studying and analyzing General Assembly resolutions on pattern of conferences, preparing tabulations of tasks to be carried out by the staff, and sending notification memoranda to concerned substantive offices.

In my administrative duty, I assisted the chief of the section in coordinating the preparation of the Performance Appraisal System (PAS) process for the period 1996–1997, in which I prepared five dialogue sheets for the periodic discussions between the section's supervisors and their staff, and the relevant periodic draft correspondence on the implementation of the PAS process.

These were the dimensions in which I performed as administrative officer for servicing conferences in Vienna, at the end of which the chief of our section gave a very impressive appraisal of my performance.

I was surely happy with the high praises for my achievements with conference services in Vienna. They were all perfectly true, and equalled those I had received from my previous offices. But I was sadly disappointed that these praises of performance were not matched with commensurate rewards.

Naturally, in keeping with the administrative practices of the organization, staff members were rewarded for good performance with career promotion to a higher level. This administrative rule of justice was not consistently applied in my situation, despite all the praises for my exceptional performances as a visually-impaired staff member. 'The pessimist' was all the time at work to block my roads to excel in my professional career with the Organization.

When I initially obtained employment with the UN, I was never under any illusions that I had finally won the battle against the pessimist. Despite my physical disability,

I had decisively defeated the pessimist in the fierce battle. But the so-called pessimist did not completely surrender to my victory. He continued to insidiously chase after me in whichever office I was working for the organization. He cunningly hid his identity in various individuals and applied all kinds of heinous tricks to undermine my career advancement.

In practice, the pessimist only pretended to be a genuine professional colleague, a sympathetic friend, a supporter of the policy promulgated by the UN on the employment of disabled persons. These were all but deceit. In fact, in his overall covert attitude, he was never sincere to the openly declared convictions of the organization as 'equal opportunities employer'.

Poor me, I was the only one to observe and suffer these skilfully manipulated behaviours of the woeful pessimist. I was serenely resilient to his unfair treatment, and he was diligently crafty to avoid exposure of his deeds.

Now totally frustrated and disillusioned with the pessimist, his mean practices and manoeuvring, which were based on irrational prejudices, I decided to approach the secretary-general directly at the UN Headquarters in New York. I wrote a confidential letter to him introducing my employment situation in Vienna through his spokesman.

At first, I was highly gratified when the spokesman replied and promised that he would pass on my letter to the secretary-general as I requested. But my joy was short lived as I quickly thereafter received a follow-up letter from the spokesman, in which he informed me that he hesitated to bring my letter to the attention of the secretary-general, given how busy he was. But he promised to store my confidential message with the secretary-general's office, and wished me the best of luck.

Although I was somehow surprised at the contents of the spokesman's response, I did not despair. I was convinced that there must be some subtle administrative communications going on between the Vienna office and UN Headquarters New York on my behalf, about which I was initially not supposed to know. Besides, it had always been the position of New York that the Vienna office should best take care of my situation. So I politely replied to the spokesman's letter in the following UN diplomatic style:

> Many thanks for the kind attention which you have given to my request. I sincerely hope you will still always remember me and my expressed concern, especially at any available relaxed and opportune moment, in view of the secretary-general's heavy and superlative workload.

> As a disabled staff member, I humbly pledge always to continue to give to the Organization the best of my talents and abilities on behalf of the Secretary-General.

> With best regards, Smart Eze.

Apart from these lively communications with the Office of the Secretary-General in New York, nothing else worth mentioning happened until the end of 1997 that could move my quest for career promotion forward. But in early 1998, I booked an appointment to see the new director-general of the UN Office at Vienna and the executive director of the UN Office on Drugs Control and Crime Prevention.

The executive director of the UN Office on Drugs

Control and Crime Prevention had only just been in office for a little over four months. His appointment had taken effect in September 1997. His office swiftly granted my request for appointment with him.

My subsequent meeting with the director-general was very cordial and highly professional. From the nature of our discussions, in which he summoned his chief of cabinet to join, I sensed that he was more excited than me for our meeting as he must have been seeing my guide dog and me from the distance in the building. He listened sympathetically to my grudges and complaints.

At the end of our meeting, he assured me that justice must be done. When I returned to my office that day, I felt very satisfied with the reception the director-general had given me. So I wrote a confidential letter to him recapitulating the main contents of our discussion.

In July 1998, I was promptly transferred to the UN Office on Drugs control and Crime Prevention (UNODCCP). What a long tongue twister! But it had a significant history behind it. Originally, the office was known as the UN International Drugs control Programme (UNDCP). When CSDHA became defunct in 1993 and its programmes were transferred to New York, one of them, the Crime Prevention and Criminal Justice Branch (CPCJB) remained behind in Vienna and was attached to UNDCP and was renamed the Centre for International Crime Prevention.

In his report of 1997 on 'Renewing the UN: A Programme for Reform', the secretary-general proposed to consolidate the work of the UN under a unified Office of Drug Control and Crime Prevention, so as to effectively counter the menaces of crime, drugs, and terrorism in society. His proposal was swiftly adopted by the General Assembly. The working relationship between these two programmes was institutionally sealed, and Vienna automatically became the nucleus of UN activities in these fields.

Now, for the sake of clarity, the UN Office for Drug Control and Crime Prevention (ODCCP) consisted of the UN International Drug Control Programme (UNDCP) and the Centre for International Crime Prevention (CICP). ODCCP was established in November 1997 to enable the organization to focus on and enhance its capacity to address the interrelated issues of drug control, crime prevention, and international terrorism in all its forms.

The director-general consulted all staff members to come up with suggestions for a matching name for the newly-consolidated office. We all suggested several wonderful names, which were highly debated. But at the end, the director-general enthusiastically settled for the office name with the acronym UNODCCP which, according to him, judiciously reflected the logical synergy that had taken place between the two programmes in Vienna.

But first, my move to the location of my new office in the building was very simple and straight forward. The offices of conference services were located in the C-Building, and those of UNODCCP were in the D- and E-Buildings. So it was not a big deal for Nico (or Niky as I often called him) and me to quickly get accustomed to the new environment of my office on the fourteenth floor in the E-Building.

Like the birds in the sky, Nicky and I had been used to migrating from one end of the building to the other. My offices were located in the D- and E-Buildings when I first began working for the organization. It was from this very part of the building that Nicky and I moved to the G-Building, where the offices of UNIS Vienna were located. Given the mammoth structure of the UNO City, it was quite a distance to walk from one end of the building to the other (that is from E- to the G-Building). It usually took Nicky and me about ten minutes to do the journey, even on six legs.

I realized that my redeployment to UNODCCP located me in the place from where I would definitely be saying goodbye to the organization in a not-too-distant future. It also meant that my long-standing wish to be returned back to the operational programmes of UNOV had been fulfilled. My post was classified as UNDCP civil affairs officer in the External Relations Unit, which was a part of the Office of the Executive-Director.

My primary duty was to act as the focal point for relations with non-governmental organizations (NGOs) and civil society organizations (CSOs), to participate in the formulation and review of guidelines for UNDCP relations with these organizations, and to represent UNDCP in meetings and conferences with NGOs.

These kinds of duty were not unfamiliar to me, given my previous work experience. I had every possible skill to meet the challenges of the new job. And, most significantly, my access technology devices had all been fully upgraded, making it possible for me to work more independently in a highly automated working environment like UNODCCP.

When I finally settled down in my office for my new job, I first reviewed UNDCP's relations with NGOs at all levels. I analyzed the previous and current trends and the results achieved in the relationship with the NGOs. These initial actions helped me to identify the prevailing and the potential areas of cooperation with these organizations at the national, regional, and international levels.

I wrote several project proposals in that regard. Two of them were to organize the Second NGO World Forum on Drug Demand Reduction in Vienna in collaboration with the Vienna NGO Committee on Narcotic Drugs, and a symposium of NGOs on drug demand reduction in Africa. The objective of these conferences was to mobilize and promote the capacity building of civil society and NGOs in the fight against drug abuse in the community, and to contribute to strengthening partnerships with UNDCP and other non-state actors in the field.

But I was terribly disappointed that many of my project proposals were never implemented. A number of lame excuses, such as chronic financial constraints, were given, but only to mollify my protests and anger. Notwithstanding, my efforts received a favourable appraisal, and were unanimously considered to be very successful and highly professional initiatives.

In my duties as the NGO focal point, I was naturally placed in a strategic position for coordinating operational activity with other units. I worked closely with the Fund-raising Unit and the Operational Branch for replenishing the fund from the Drug Abuse Prevention Centre (DAPC), Tokyo, and for awarding specific projects to selected NGOs. I particularly enjoyed this activity because the DAPC fund was a very successful scheme. It was so well known around the world that we received more grant proposals than we could possibly fund.

The DAPC fund, popularly known as 'NGO helping NGO' was an initiative in support of the UN Decade Against Drug Abuse (1991–2000). The Japanese NGO, the Drug Abuse Prevention Centre (DAPC)/Tokyo, organized annual public campaigns throughout the country. The aim was to increase awareness among young Japanese of the dangers of drug abuse, and to raise money for UNDCP to support the work of NGOs around the world.

Thousands of youth participated in street collections throughout the country. Each year DAPC selected eight of these volunteers who had been particularly effective in the campaign and designated them as Young Civic Ambassadors. The group travelled to Vienna to hand over the contributions to the UNDCP executive director. I was so impressed by the enthusiasm and professionalism with which the nationwide fund-raising campaigns were carried out in Japan. This prompted me to explore possible ways in which the scheme could be replicated elsewhere.

I was barely one year in my new job when, in 1999, the Austrian government, the City of Vienna, and our office jointly created the UN Vienna Civil Society Award. The purpose of the award was to honour individuals, institutions, and organizations that helped to fight global crime and drug abuse and foster justice and social progress. The award consisted of a medal, a certificate, as well as prize money.

Organizing the event was not a simple matter. It kept me busy all through until the day of the ceremony awards. First, I prepared a consolidated draft list of NGOs that collaborated with UNODCCP, and distributed it to the appropriate units at headquarters and the field offices. Then, I updated the criteria for the selection of qualified NGOs, and circulated the invitation for nominations.

In the meantime, I conducted arrangements for the establishment of a selection committee and the selection of the winners. To ensure the smooth running of the events, I worked intensely with the responsible Austrian authorities for the final arrangements of the award ceremony at the festivity hall of the Vienna municipality.

But, as I collected and researched information materials to prepare various kinds of briefing notes and speeches, I particularly enjoyed writing the bi-annual reports on UNDCP collaboration with NGOs to the Commission on Narcotic Drugs. I had the privilege of writing and submitting three of these reports to the commission in 2001, 2003, and 2005 before my separation from service. I filled each report with the information I had received from the field offices, NGOs, and other civil society organizations in a letter which I circulated to them earlier before the meeting of the commission.

In reviewing the cooperation of other UN organizations with NGOs and civil CSOs, I analyzed the prevailing trends and results achieved. One of my unique activities in that respect was to liaise with the Non-governmental Liaison Service (NGLS) in terms of the support it provided in disseminating the activities of UNDCP. I attended regularly the NGLS Programme and Coordination meetings, held annually in Geneva, Switzerland.

I participated in the lively discussions in which the policies and activities of NGLS were shaped and evaluated, given that UNDCP was one of the UN agencies and programmes that provided financial support to NGLS. But, when I took on the responsibility of coordinating our work with NGLS, I first had to convince the sceptics in our office as to the rationale for continuing UNDCP financial contributions.

I vehemently argued that the benefits of our contributions to NGLS were worthwhile, given that NGLS's information outreach regularly covered the role, work, experiences, and policies of our office and the issues of particular concern to us. Finally, I succeeded with my argument, and the financial contributions of our office to NGLS were continued, and even increased from their previous levels.

My first attendance at those meetings in 1999 provided me an excellent opportunity to hold working sessions with NGLS staff members. Of particular importance were my discussions with the NGLS senior coordinator, in which we explored the various ways to maximize services to UNDCP. I also conducted individual consultations with colleagues from other agencies to exchange mutual experience and practical approaches in our day-to-day dealings with NGOs and CSOs. These consultations reciprocally proved useful to everyone since, like me, most of the colleagues had only just been appointed to the job of NGO affairs in their respective agencies.

Travelling to Geneva every year at the end of winter to attend these meetings quickly became a routine activity for me. I encountered few or no difficulties at all in my numerous journeys between Vienna and Geneva. At all stages of my travels, I applied my skills as a typhlonaut to the full. I was always meticulously organized both before my travels and at my arrivals at my hotel in Geneva. It was a lot of fun for me as a UN expert, and especially as a typhlonaut.

But the only time I could not participate in an NGLS Programme and Coordination meeting was in 2002, when it was held at the UN Headquarters in New York rather than in Geneva. Following the terrorist passenger aircraft attacks on the United States of America on 11 September 2001, there was a temporary sharp drop in air travel around the world. As I could not travel to New York at this time, a staff member of our liaison office at UN Headquarters was requested to attend the NGLS meeting there in my place.

In May 2002, there was a sudden change in the management of UNODCCP. A new director-general of UNOV and executive-director of UNODCCP had been appointed. What a long title for a name! It had always been known like that, since the two functions were combined at the post of under secretary-general.

When the new director-general arrived, he considered the name 'UNODCCP' to be too long and too difficult to pronounce. He decided to simplify it. This time, the change of name was not accomplished in a democratic process. The director-general did not seek the opinion of the staff at large. He simply adopted a new name for the programme within his office.

Arriving in the office one day, we were informed that the name of our programme had been changed from

UNODCCP to UNODC, meaning UN Office on Drugs and Crime. Everyone in the office was astonished at the new name because of its linguistic connotation. Anyway, we all soon became accustomed to referring to our office as UNODC instead of UNODCCP.

But even on one of my missions to Geneva to attend the NGLS Policy and Coordination meetings, several colleagues from other UN agencies approached me curiously and told me that the new name of our office somehow seemed to be misleading. Some said they found the meaning, at least in the English language, very funny.

In the meantime, I had learned my lesson when my very first guide dog suddenly passed away and I was left for months and months without one. So I decided to have another fully trained guide dog with me when Nicko retired. But a few months before Nicko's tenth birthday, when he was officially due to retire, the trainer informed me that the replacement dog had unexpectedly developed a unique character and had to be taken out of training and disqualified.

For many years, Nicko had been suffering from Lyme borreliosis, which was thought to have originated from an infection caused by a bite from a tick that was infected with Lyme bacteria. But our veterinary doctor treated him successfully with antibiotics. The medication was administered to him each year so that the illness would not reoccur with chronic infection, pains, tiredness, blurry vision, and neurological problems, some of which could affect his thinking.

But one morning in January 2003, when we arrived by train in the city at the Westbahnhof train station, on our way to the office, Nicko could not get up as usual. Only with repeated encouragement was he able to get up and guide me to the office. He was taken immediately to the doctor that morning. After the check-up, the doctor diagnosed poor Nicko with malignant cancer of the liver in an advanced stage. He said it was known as "'eighty-day cancer'" because of its speed and ferocity. It could not have been detected when Nicko had his blood tested three months earlier.

This wicked cancer was so bad that no clinical surgery could help whatsoever. So, seven days later, my poor guide dog Nicko passed away. Nicky died exactly on my birthday. I had to abandon any thoughts of birthday celebrations. I was unimaginably devastated, emotionally and physically.

In May 2003, the trainer finally delivered a new and fully trained guide dog to me. But, for a good three months without a guide dog, I had fairly managed my daily journeys from home in Eichgraben to the office at the Vienna International Centre very well. I resorted to my basic navigation skills of using the white cane and the relay system. Of course, I missed the intelligence and dependability of my guide dog.

My new guide dog was a yellow Labrador retriever. Like the other dogs, he was young, very beautiful, and exceptionally intelligent. He was my first Labrador guide dog. His name was Nello, but I also called him 'Yellow Nello' as a nickname whenever I wanted to tease him.

Like his predecessors, Nello quickly mastered the route of our daily journeys from our home to the office. Within a short period, he guided me to anywhere in the labyrinth of buildings of the Vienna International Centre. Even in the city of Vienna, he negotiated our routes superbly through the streets, roads, cars, people, objects, and crossings.

After we had worked together for three months, Nello took the compulsory guide dog qualification test as mandated by the law in Austria. The test was conducted before an examination board with representatives from the sponsoring agencies. Nello's performance was excellent, and he scored the highest marks and received his certificate as a fully trained guide dog.

I was very happy to have had the opportunity to help our office to actively involve the NGOs and the civil society in our numerous activities. Through my skills of coordination and persuasion, our office secured the participation of these specialized and experienced organizations in the planning and execution of well-defined projects with funding from UNDCP. Our office worked globally with these organizations as executing agencies, consultants, beneficiaries, and donors in drug demand reduction. We maintained dialogue with members of the Vienna NGO Committee on Narcotic Drugs, the New York NGO Committee on Substance Abuse, as well as similar organizations at the national level through their participation in our meetings and events on drug issues.

With my long experience and professionalism, I could help our office provide a range of services to these organizations from our office headquarters in Vienna or from the field offices. These services included strengthening the capacity of these organizations in developing countries and countries in transition with ad hoc grants to help them deliver services to their constituencies. Our office was also able to facilitate networking among these organizations, to publish information on their activities, and to provide educational information, advice, and promotional materials for distribution.

I was so glad to have succeeded in setting up a reciprocal information flow between our office and these organizations. This state of affairs greatly enhanced our overall working relations with their international umbrella establishments. One such establishment was the Vienna NGO Committee on Narcotic Drugs. I worked closely with its leadership on a daily basis and facilitated the holding of its regular meetings and other events at the Vienna International Centre.

I never failed to take part in any of those meetings, which were held at least four times in a calendar year. I provided briefings on UNDCP activities to the participants. Thereafter, I reported back to our office on the proceedings of the meetings and highlighted the decisions taken by the committee, which might have programmatic implications for UNDCP.

One duty I passionately enjoyed most of the time was maintaining and updating the UNDCP NGO Database in Drug Demand Reduction, and preparing the periodic publications of the UNDCP Directory of NGOs Working in Drug Demand Reduction. With the assistance of various interns at different times and a junior professional staff, I succeeded in preparing and publishing three editions of the directory, posting them up on UNDCP intranet and Internet pages.

It was a highly demanding and extremely work-intensive task, to which I devoted much of my time and energy, supervising and organizing the work on the directory until its final production and distribution. I applied a similar working procedure in the maintenance of the NGO database, as it was intractably linked to the NGO directory.

Despite these achievements I made in UNDCP working relations with the NGOs and the CSOs, it was clear to me that there were still grounds to be covered for further improvements. So I left behind with our office proposals on some future actions to improve working relations with these organizations. These actions included:

o To establish focal points of these organizations in each field office, and to foster good relations between them and governments;

o To focus not only on large, well-known CSOs/
NGOs but to seek out more non-specialized
organizations;

o To intensify efforts to promote the formation of
country and regional networks, and to use them
to encourage these organizations with particular
expertise to share it with others;

o To evaluate periodically the activities of these
organizations, so as to identify successful
approaches, to avoid duplication and waste of
resources;

o To establish recommended strategies, concepts
and methods, which merited replication, and
to prepare a catalogue of resource materials
generated by projects which could be shared and
added for local use;

o To streamline the administration of funds to
these organizations by delegating responsibility
for the approval of project proposals to field
offices, where possible.

Truly, I had my dream for the mainstream employment
fulfilled by having worked so successfully for the UN. I had
triumphed over the pessimist and proved him wrong in all his
scepticisms. I quickly became very popular in the entire UN
family and beyond, a phenomenon which was judiciously
recognized by the staff and management at the Vienna
International Centre.

I was elected to the Staff Council in Vienna, in which,

as a staff representative, I contributed to identifying, examining, and resolving issues relating to staff welfare, and rapidly acquiring extensive knowledge on matters relating to contracts, pensions, post adjustments, job classifications, health insurance, and organizational structure.

For ten years, until my retirement from the organization, I was nominated by the secretary-general to serve as one of the seven members of the Panel on Discrimination and Other Grievances at the UN Office in Vienna. Our panel investigated grievances submitted by staff members arising from their employment with the organization. Such grievances included, but were not limited to, allegations of discriminatory treatment in the workplace.

In principle, we always first sought to resolve the grievances by informal means. Where this proved impossible, we recommended a formal investigation to the secretary-general. One marathon investigation we conducted was about the conditions of service in one of the departments with a staff of over 120. We interviewed and contacted by letter a total number of 105 staff members, which represented 95 percent of the total workforce of that department. Our investigation was based on an agreed methodology, in which we applied a standardized questionnaire to ensure that all interviews were carried out in a comparable manner to yield results that were useful for a comprehensive analysis.

I was nominated by the staff council to serve as expert on the UNOV and UNIDO Joint Administrative Standing Committee on Medical and Life Insurance, which had a membership of six representatives of staff and management. I held this position also for ten years until my retirement.

As technical experts, we monitored and evaluated the performance of the contract on the group medical insurance with J. Van Breda and Company International, reviewing the premium monthly rates of medical expenses based on a comparison of the monthly premiums paid and the reimbursements received by participants over a twelve-month period.

If the amount of reimbursements made in a reviewing period of one year did not exceed the premiums paid in the same period, we recommended no changes in the premium rates of the plan. Otherwise, the premiums were adjusted accordingly.

These were some of the indelible highlights of my career with the UN, which had begun in October 1980 in Vienna. This wonderful journey had taken me through various professional landscapes of the organization. My accomplishments were so numerous that, with all good intent and purposes, I could not enumerate and describe all of them in a single trait.

But suffice it to say that I heaved a sigh of deep relief and had a tremendous feeling of satisfaction as I experienced and digested those glamorous farewell ceremonies on my behalf in the office in that month of February in 2005. I was so proud of the achievements of my meritorious services to the UN, which was now finally crowned with a happy ending.

The signing out procedure from the office for me was very simple, thanks to the advances in modern office automated computer technology. It was a standard clearance procedure, which every staff member performed when separating from service to the organization. It took only a few days for the various relevant offices to clear me of being in possession of any property belonging to the organization. I was so happy that everything went quickly and flawlessly, and the release of my last month's salary in service was not delayed after my departure.

I was pensive as the VIC Buildings Management workers moved my personal belongings from my office on the fourteenth floor of the D-Building to our family car waiting in the garage downstairs. My secretary spent days helping me to arrange and stuff all my personal belongings into different cartons, which we carefully labelled according to their contents.

Clearing my office desk and sorting out my personal effects was not an easy task. I decided on the things to take with me, those to leave behind, and the ones to discard to the waste bin. Among them were hard-copy files and numerous diskettes, in which I stored important personal information on the various landscapes of my career journey with the UN. There were also various adaptive electronic devices, both current and outdated, flower vases, plants, and artifices with which I decorated my office wherever I settled down in my career journey.

As the last batches of my personal belongings were moved out from my office, I dressed Nello up in his harness and walked over to my neighbours in their offices on both sides of the corridors to say goodbye. It was a very emotional moment for me.

When I arrived at our family car in the garage, I turned around to face the building and reflected deeply on how it had all once begun for me. I immediately remembered how I overcame the first hurdle of catching up with my ambitions with a doctorate degree at the University of Vienna. And right there, like a thunderbolt, I remembered the concluding phrase by the presenter of an Austrian television pre-retirement documentary film about me in November 2003, in which he said, 'Smart has made it!'

Catching Up With ambition

The ceremony hall of the main building of the Vienna University was filled up on that day with guests walking and talking from all directions. There were a lot of noises as people chatted, greeted, and hugged each other. From my perspective—being only able to hear and not see—it was like being in a hive of millions of restless but happy bees. I was pretty sure that even some of my own personal guests were among them.

I had arrived in the ceremony hall with my wife Renate and our little daughter Esther. But I had to leave them shortly after they had taken their seats in order to join the other graduates in the designated area. It was Thursday, 20 December 1979. It was my graduation day from the Vienna University, and, indeed, with all humility, a unique occasion for me.

There were twenty-four of us in number to receive our doctoral awards on that day, and to be ushered into the academic world. We were seated in two rows, facing the audience. I was the only visually impaired and black African graduate among them. Like the other graduates, I was meticulously dressed up in a dapper suit. The dean of academic affairs of our university and other officials sat diagonally opposite us to the right, ready to officiate the occasion.

I listened excitedly as the orchestra played the universally acclaimed international students' anthem, 'De Brevitate Vitae' (On the Shortness of Life). Automatically, the words came into my mind: '*Gaudeamus igitur, Juvenes dum sumus…*' (Let us rejoice therefore while we are young…). My heart pounded as I silently joined the orchestra in singing, '*Vivat academia, Vivant professores…*' (Long live the academy! Long live the teachers!…). *What a very solemn occasion!* I thought to myself.

When the speeches and rituals were all over, each of us was called up one after the other to receive our doctorate diploma, which was ceremoniously handed over personally by the dean of academic affairs. The texts were written in the Latin language on a papyrus roll that was decorated with the big seal of the University of Vienna. When it was my turn, I walked straight up to the dean of academic affairs, who was flanked on both sides by two other university officials, and proudly received from him my doctorate diploma. He shook my hand and congratulated me, and so did the other two university officials.

After the official graduation ceremony, I got up quickly from my seat and walked across to greet my guests in the hall, carrying my papyrus roll firmly, but tenderly, under my arm. I had joyously invited many guests to the occasion. And many of them had turned up to wish me well. Among them were friends and fellow students and family relations. As I walked in their midst, I held my diploma high for everyone to see. I shook hands and greeted each of them, and thanked them for coming to share in my joy that day and for all times.

But, among my many guests, I had missed one exceptional well-wisher who had decided to remain anonymous. The only information I had about him was that he was an Iranian citizen. He had heard and read about me and my successful completion, as a blind man, of my university studies with a doctorate degree. He had congratulated me earlier in writing before the graduation day for my remarkable achievement. As a token of goodwill, he generously gave me a substantial amount of cash money through the Austrian Society for the War Blind.

On leaving the university building complex, I stopped briefly on the steps of the ceremony hall. I turned round to face the entrance and reflected deeply on my determination to catch up with the ambitions that had escaped me for so many years through no fault of mine. I calculated that it had taken me, so far, ten years, seven months, and eighteen days since my arrival in Austria to achieve these ambitions, which today included my acquisition of a doctorate degree from the University of Vienna.

On Friday, 2 May 1969, our aircraft landed at the Vienna International Airport. It was around eight o'clock in the evening. The aircraft belonged to the International Committee of the Red Cross (ICRC). It had flown us from Cotonou in the Republic of Benin to Vienna in Austria.

But, twenty-four hours earlier, an ICRC small cargo plane had flown us out of Biafra in a dangerous night flight from the Uli-Ihiala provisional airport. It was a very risky operation for the pilots and the passengers, because the Federal Military Government of Nigeria had tightly blockaded Biafra in the air, at sea and on land. After the self-proclaimed Republic of Biafra had seceded from Nigeria in 1967, the Nigerian-Biafran War, also known as the Nigerian Civil War, had been horrific and bloody.

The heroic young Canadian pilots braved the blockades to deliver humanitarian aids and relief to the starving population of Biafra on behalf of the ICRC. They were always fired at in the air and on the ground on their humanitarian missions by the Nigerian army, even though their small cargo planes were clearly marked with the Red Cross insignia. The Nigerian war machinery did not respect the distinct mission of ICRC as an impartial, neutral, and independent organization whose exclusively humanitarian mission was to protect the lives and dignity of victims of armed conflict and other situations of violence and to provide them with assistance.

As we were being rescued and flown out of Biafra from the Uli-Ihiala Airport that night, our Red Cross cargo plane was shot at several times from beneath. Luckily, the raining bullets could not penetrate through the bottom of the plane because it had been unsophisticatedly, but very skilfully, protected with thick planks of wood. We all huddled together, held each other's hands, and prayed so hard for the Lord's protection as the shots of the guns were continuously fired at our small plane as we flew over Nigerian territory along the Atlantic coastline, over Lagos, and to Cotonou in the Republic of Benin.

In Cotonou, we were transferred from the small cargo plane to a bigger and stronger plane which was suited for intercontinental flights. It was carrying a large number of refugees, who had been rescued from Biafra. The majority of them were wounded Biafran soldiers, and I was one of their number. Sjouke Bakker, the young Red Cross medical doctor from the Netherlands and a few nurses accompanied the refugees all the way from the hot land of Biafra.

The plane left Cotonou very early in the morning on 2 May 1969, flying the wounded Biafran soldiers to different countries in Europe for medical treatment. Stops were to be made in Switzerland, West Germany, Finland, Norway, Denmark, Sweden, and Netherlands.

Ten of us disembarked from the plane in Vienna, Austria. We were eight Biafran soldiers with horrible bullet wounds in our mouths, jaws, noses, and eyes, and two were non-combatants with injuries also to their eyes.

When our plane arrived at the Vienna International Airport, our hosts were already at hand to welcome us. They boarded the plane and searched for us among the other passengers, who continued their journey to the other European countries. It was a hectic moment and a moving scene on the plane as we chatted loudly, hugged, and parted from each other with sincere wishes for a successful treatment.

Two of our Austrian hosts snapped me up and carried me on their shoulders out of the plane. In this manner we passed through the airport customs and security and then to the VIP lounge, where the other members of the welcoming party had assembled. As they welcomed us, I felt their friendship and generosity, and their joy and relief at our ultimate rescue. We were served delicious European meals and allowed to rest for a while.

Our welcoming hosts at the airport were members of the Austrian National Red Cross, representatives of the Municipality of the city of Vienna, members of the Austrian Biafra Committee, made up of groups of friends of Biafra and Biafran Students in Austria. As in several other European countries, the Municipality of the City of Vienna had responded to the pathetic appeal by the International Committee of the Red Cross to the international committee for help to rescue millions of the Biafran people from persistent starvation and massacre in the on-going civil war in Nigeria.

Acting on behalf of the entire population of Austria, the Vienna Municipality invited ten of us as its official guests to receive medical treatment in the city. The sufferings of the people of Biafra were universally publicized in Europe. The lamentable pictures of malnourished children, suffering and dying from the horrible disease known as *kwashiorkor* were prominently reported in news media. This malnutrition disease, suffered mainly by Biafran children, was caused by severe protein and vitamin deficiency and was characterized by retarded growth, changes in pigmentation, potbelly, and anaemia. *Biafrakind* was a new word used all over Europe to described the condition of these children. The word quickly became popular in everyday usage in practically all the European languages, and is still used today.

Just like many others in Europe, the people of Austria could not possibly sit back and watch these terribly disgusting scenes shown on their televisions and written about and illustrated in their newspapers day in day out, without offering some kind of help. Consequently, the Municipality of the city of Vienna promptly initiated and implemented the humanitarian action, by which we were rescued and brought to Austria for medical treatment and rehabilitation.

After we had eaten our meals, had a good rest, and had gathered sufficient strength to travel again, our hosts accompanied us from the airport VIP lounge to the Red Cross bus which had been waiting for us the whole evening in the parking lot of the airport building complex. We entered the bus and were driven straight to the Lainz Medical Hospital, located in the western part of Vienna.

Already that night, we had been separated into two groups in accordance with the nature of the projected medical treatment of our wounds. Six comrades with bullet wounds in their mouths, noses, and jaws were referred to the plastic and reconstructive surgery department. Four of us with eye injuries were referred to the eye clinic. After procedurally handing us over to the hospital personnel, our welcoming hosts graciously bade us good night and departed for the day.

As I lay in my sickbed in the eye clinic ward of the hospital, my heart pounded with joy. I tried very hard to understand where I was at that moment. Peace and tranquillity filled the area around me. There were no deafening and threatening sounds of artillery gunshots banging nearby and in the distance

I had no anxieties anymore about intermittent night air raids by the Nigerian warplanes that dropped bombs indiscriminately on the civilian population and public buildings, like hospitals and marketplaces during the day. I felt very safe and happy as I finally fell asleep in my sickbed. I was no longer in war-stricken and life-threatening Biafra, but right in the middle of the peaceful country of Austria. I had a very sound and deep sleep that night.

When I woke up the following morning, I revived and strengthened my long-standing expectations that I would be able to see again now that I was in Austria. When, back in the Biafran Armed forces Hospital in Ohafia, the young Red Cross doctor from the Netherlands told me that I would be going to Austria for treatment, I was filled with so many high hopes and so much happiness that the doctors would be able to restore my vision once I arrived there. I had to wait the weekend for the doctors to arrive and begin examining the conditions of my eyes. The two days seemed like ages as I waited.

In the following days and weeks, the doctors carried out different kinds of tests on my eyes. But I had a lot of apprehension after each test. One thing I did not want to happen was a failure in the efforts of the doctors. I had full trust in their professionalism and in their genuine struggle to help me regain my vision. But what a wishful thought!

One Monday morning, the inevitable happened. The

senior eye specialist of the department walked into my hospital room accompanied by his entourage of senior and junior doctors and nurses on duty. He was on his regular morning rounds to the wards to inspect and apprise himself of the condition of all the patients. He pronounced judgements on the status of the treatment of each patient, and gave instructions on the course of actions to be taken thereafter. He was a professor of ophthalmologic studies at the University of Vienna.

The professor came close to my bed and greeted me in a very friendly manner. After enquiring about how my eyes were feeling, he took my hand and held it slightly for a while. Then he said to me in a gentle voice that they would not be able to restore my sight. The wounds had been so deep and devastating that the damage they caused to my eyes was beyond any possible repairs. Therefore, at the moment, there was nothing else they could do for me.

In an attempt to reassure me, the professor cautiously speculated that perhaps something might be done about my eyes in the future. But he said that it depended wholly on how the condition of my eyes developed, as well as what new knowledge and technological advances might develop in the treatment of eye diseases. He concluded that I should rest assured that they had done everything possible to help me to see again. As I listened to him and gave him a bewildered look, the professor comforted me compassionately and shook my hand and patted me on the shoulder. He then quietly left my room with his entire entourage of doctors and nurses.

As they left me, my room sounded unusually calm and spooky and I felt so lonely and weak. I shivered with cold and was extremely frightened. I was very sad. The news from the professor had shattered all my hopes to be able to see again. All my desires to see the sunlight had been flatly dashed. I would not recover. The hope of seeing again had restrained me from voluntarily destroying my life as I lay at the Biafran Armed forces Hospital in Ohafia several months before.

Luckily, I had eaten my breakfast before the professor broke the news to me because now I had lost appetite for any food whatsoever. *Why should I eat any food?* I asked myself. *To preserve my life and live as a blind person at my age and for the rest of my life?* This was exactly what I did not want to do.

I refused to take my meals the rest of Monday and the whole of Tuesday. Each time the nurses noticed that I had neither touched nor eaten the food, they carried the cold food back to the kitchen and reported my refusal of regular meals on the journal for the doctors' appraisal.

On Tuesday evening, (at exactly eight o'clock) the deputy senior eye specialist of the department entered my room. First, she stopped at the foot of my bed and read the report of the nurses on the journal. Then she greeted me and enquired about my condition. As I recognized her voice, I said in a low level tone, "'Thank you, doctor. I am fine.'"

She moved close to my bed and gently held my hand. I could hear the smile in her voice as she said, 'No, Smart. You can't be fine like that.' But I pretended not to know what she meant. I asked, 'Why not, doctor?' 'You have not eaten any food since Monday,' she replied. 'You have been refusing your meals. You must be very hungry and weak. Why do you do that? Is it because of the outcome of the medical tests given to you yesterday?' she rightly concluded.

I turned toward her face and cried silently as I tried to gather strength to answer her questions. I thought for a while and then said, 'Yes, doctor. So I am going to be blind the rest of my life? But I thought I would be able to see again. But now…' My voice suddenly began to fade, and I could not complete the sentence. I immediately covered my face with my hands and wept.

There was silence in the room as I momentarily stopped crying. She took my right hand gently and asked me to feel one of two objects in front of her. I ran my fingers along the first one. As I was trying to think of what it could be, she asked me to feel the second one. I did so, thinking that, this time, I would understand what it was exactly. But I could not identify either of the two objects because they felt like two tiny soft round sticks, about as long as my forearm. Then she asked me, 'Do you know what they are?' I said, 'No, doctor.'

When she noticed that I had begun thinking again to guess a second time, she quickly butted in and told me bluntly that the two narrow cylindrical objects were her legs. She had suffered poliomyelitis in her childhood that caused the paralysis of her legs. But she could go to school at all levels. She even attended the university and studied medicine. Today she was the second in command of the eye clinic of this hospital. She paused for a while, as if her intension was to give me a chance to say something.

I was very surprised at what the deputy senior eye specialist had just revealed to me. As I could still not say anything, she continued, reminding me that I was now in Europe. She only told me her own story to encourage me to believe that I could have opportunities to develop my own abilities. There were a lot of opportunities over here, she said emphatically. The only things I needed were hard work, determination, endurance, and self-confidence. All these were equally important, not necessarily in that order, she concluded convincingly.

But, as I was still amazed, I managed to ask curiously, 'Doctor, but how do you come to work?' She replied that she drove in her own car to work everyday by herself. Her car was technically adapted to her needs as a physically disabled person. She operated everything in the car by using her hands.

Again, still in my astonishment, I asked, 'Doctor, but how do you move about within and outside the hospital premises? How do you carry out operations on patients in the theatre room?' At this juncture, she asked me to step out of my bed and feel the chair in which she was sitting. She explained to me that it was her battery-operated wheelchair. It enabled her to move around in the hospital, as well as in her home.

I listened intensely the whole time to her story, absorbing every word like a flash of light. I felt I was gradually regaining strength as I boldly ask, '"But, doctor, how can I read and write as I am now totally blind?' She enthusiastically answered me that there was a system of reading and writing for the blind. It was called the Braille system. She explained that, instead of using their eyes like sighted people, blind persons used their fingers to read and write texts.

I heaved a deep sigh of relief at that knowledge, but further asked her, 'But how can I write so that sighted people can read what I have written?' She told me that there was a school in the city where blind persons were taught to read and write with their fingers, as well with typewriters so that sighted people could read the texts they had written. I could be sent to that school to learn those skills as well as other things. Before leaving my room, she said assuredly, 'Remember, Smart, all you need is hard work, determination, endurance, and self-confidence.' She patted me softly on the shoulder, bade me goodnight, and departed.

Shortly after she left, I turned round in my bed and lay flat on my back with all my attention focused squarely on the ceiling of the room. My head was spinning with thoughts as I tried to organize them into a logical system. I could now sense some lively joy in me, and some kind of optimism approaching me hastily from the distance. Then I said to myself convincingly, 'Hey, Smart, you may be blind, but all is not yet lost!'

I remembered that I had vaguely heard about that system of reading and writing for the blind some time ago in Nigeria. But I had not paid attention to it because I was not interested. I never knew that it would one day be of immense relevance to me. I also remembered that I had studied touch typewriting for one year whilst I was attending a commercial institute at Aba, Nigeria, in 1961. That skill could be of great benefit to me today as blind person, as I would be able to write texts that sighted people could read.

I continued meditating as if I were in an autogenic (autosuggestion) training motion. But I fell into a deep sleep without notice, as I recalled later. I had numerous terrifying but pleasant nightmares in my sleep. When I encountered obstacles in my dream, such as cars, lorries, deep groves on the ground, or dangerous situations, like guns and shootings on the war front, I noticed I could fly over them like a bird. I could move freely without fears in my dreams.

It came to me like a thunderbolt in the morning when I woke up. I felt mentally enriched and physically strengthened, even though I had not eaten any food in several days. But I was extremely hungry. I had so much appetite, and was now prepared to accept my meals. I had not been as happy and confident of myself since I lost my sight.

As usual, the nurse on duty brought my breakfast to me in my room. I consumed it quickly with an unprecedented appetite. Then I asked for more food, which the nurse happily brought to me. I could sense her body movement, which conveyed that she was surprised that I had begun to accept my breakfast rather than refusing it. I finished the second ration of the breakfast with lots of ease, which prompted the nurse to ask if I wanted some more. I thanked and told her that the breakfast was delicious and I had had sufficient for the moment. I could tell she was relieved at last as she left my room.

I had absorbed the dialogue with the deputy senior eye specialist of the department the previous night as if it were a delicious food. The information she had provided, and her encouragement, had helped me to see the light again clearly with the 'mind's eye'. I realized that, from now on, I must accept my condition as a reality in order to move forward. In short, I must accept the status quo of my blindness now and always.

As a Christian, I was convinced that I did not become blind because my God was a wicked one. My God would never give me a load that was too heavy for me, because he would always give me the strength to carry it.

I humbly believed that my God simply wanted to bring his message of love and forgiveness to the whole humanity through my blindness. I concluded each of my prayers with this true personal wish, 'Oh, God, show your light through me to the world in all situations!'

I resolved to meet the challenges of my new life with the mind's eye. But I recognized that, as I moved forward, I would gradually discover the powers of the mind's eye. Until now, I had never consciously thought of using the powers of the mind's eye in my sighted life. I was quite satisfied with the abundant visual abilities that I had. Whenever I was offered the option of perceiving with the mind's eye, I quickly brushed it aside, and chose the visual solution, as it was easier and more obvious.

I thought that if I were congenitally blind, the power of the mind's eye could be part and parcel of my life. I would not worry about anything else, because it would be available to me all the time. But as adventitiously blind, I must learn how to apply it in all my undertakings if I was going to succeed in the sighted world. Having seen before could be an advantage for me to compensate for the abilities which I might miss had I been born blind. I cheered myself up with the maxim that 'every disappointment is a blessing'.

One sunny morning in June, a lady walked into my room and greeted me in a friendly manner. As I responded to her greeting, she came straight to the side of my bed. I immediately observed from her voice and movement that she was not one of the nurses. She introduced herself to me by her first name 'Dietlinde' and quickly added her surname 'Dörfler' thereafter. I could tell she was smiling. 'I come from the Social Welfare Department of the Municipality of the City of Vienna. I am a social counsellor, and I am going to be responsible for your welfare in our country,' she said.

When she finished introducing herself, she asked me a couple of questions, which were more conversational than one might expect from an interview. I felt very relaxed in our conversation and opened myself up happily, and was ready to cooperate with her to help me. I was especially filled with joy to know that I had someone like her to help me in sorting out my new life at this crucial stage. She was compassionate and highly professional.

I was amazed at the speed with which, in a single visit, she could appraise my state of mind and obtain my confidence. She was a young lady, barely five years older than me, and had been married for only a few weeks. She understood my situation correctly, and was like an elder sister to me, something that I cherished very much at that point, as I had no friends or relatives to turn to in a foreign country.

My new helper walked me in a gingerly manner into the garden of the hospital and showed me all of the plants and flowers. I was a little insecure standing firmly on my feet because my equilibrium was still compromised by my blindness. I touched the plants gently, and smelled the flowers.

It was a beautiful experience for me. For the first time, I had instinctively applied the power of the mind's eye to appreciate the nature around me. I had not been in Europe before I became blind. Consequently, I was unfamiliar with what the environment and the people might look like. All that I knew about Europe and the inhabitants had come to me only by way of films, books, and pictures.

I knew pretty well that I would continue to discover more ways to manoeuvre in the world as I moved forward in my new way of living. I would not need to fly as I had in my dream in order to overcome obstacles in the real world. I would develop skills in the use of my other senses to excel and survive in life.

As my social counsellor assisted me to explore more of the beauties of the garden, she revealed to me that a teacher for the blind in the city would come to visit me. He would introduce more of these skills, as well as the basics of the Braille writing and reading system to me. The Municipality of the City of Vienna would send me to the school for the blind in the city, where I would be taught those skills in detail.

A few days later, I was transferred to the geriatric department of the hospital. The doctors at the eye clinic did not have any more treatments for me. The medical tests of my eyes were completed, and the results were known. But I always went back to them for periodic checkups of my eyesight from my new lodging.

I understood fully that my lodging with the older people was temporary because it was vacation period and the school for the blind in the city was closed until September. But having been approached by my social counsellor from the City of Vienna, one of the teachers at the blind school kindly volunteered to tutor me during the vacation period at the hospital.

The volunteer teacher came to me twice weekly to teach me reading and writing in Braille as well as basic mobility skills. On top of that, I had to learn German! He was so nice and extremely patient with me as I initially struggled to learn to pronounce the German words. But somehow my knowledge of the English language was a big help for me.

I curiously observed that some words in both English and German sounded nearly the same to my ears, and their meanings were closely related. But I soon found out that I should not take these characteristics for granted when learning to speak and write the German language. One morning, I proudly and independently found my way to the hospital kiosk to buy a packet of milk. I really enjoyed drinking fresh milk, which we were always served once a day at the hospital. I checked out the exact pronunciation of the word *milk* with one of the nurses, and I studiously memorized the pronunciation. When I got to the kiosk, I noticed a long queue of customers waiting and rushing to buy different grocery items. When it got to my turn, the kiosk attendant wanted to know what I wanted to purchase. Flustered, I remembered that what I wanted sounded similar to *milk* in English. I mumbled something that the kiosk attendant could not understand right away. He became impatient with me, and I immediately was restless. I knew precisely what I wanted to purchase. So I said 'moo moo moo', and snapped and sucked in the air with my lips, like a calf sucking milk from its mother's breast. Then the kiosk attendant said, 'Oh yes, you want milk.'

I was very embarrassed when I finally got my milk from the kiosk attendant. As I negotiated my way back to my area of the hospital, I reminded myself that I would have to master the proper pronunciation of German words. The German language was the only means through which I could communicate with the people around me. Certainly, if I were not blind, I could have simply pointed at the milk on the shelves to tell the kiosk attendant what I actually wanted to purchase from him.

My living in the geriatric ward of the hospital did not make much difference to me at all, as I was now more resolved than ever to meet the challenges ahead. I calculated that over 99 percent of the residents staying with me in the home at that point were over sixty years old. The oldest were almost one hundred years old. Many of them could not at any time get off their beds, and therefore required constant attention by the nurses.

I was the youngest among the residents. There was one man who was a little over forty years of age. He was suffering from some mental disorders. But his mental state appeared to be sufficiently stable to permit him to run some daily errands for the older residents, such as purchasing items for them from the hospital kiosk, which he enthusiastically did.

Our rooms were as large as the wards in a hospital hall. There were many residents in my ward. The beds were arranged in columns on either side of a long corridor, and there were wide spaces between the beds, which ensured unimpaired movement of the residents and the nurses on duty at any time. There were a cabinet and a little locker between the beds on one end for storing the belongings of each resident.

I lay between two very old men as my neighbours. One of them was so nice to me that he always freely gave money to the 'errand resident' to purchase items for me from the hospital kiosk. He was, for me, the 'papa' as I habitually called him.

I was pleasantly surprised one afternoon when I heard the voice of the deputy senior eye specialist of the eye clinic in my ward. I recognized her voice instantly because she called out my name as she propelled her wheelchair towards my bed. We exchanged greetings politely, and she enquired about my well-being and how I was coping with the new environment.

While she moved her wheelchair towards my bed, I noticed that she was accompanied by someone. She took my hand gently and told me that she had brought someone to introduce to me. I became curious, but waited patiently to hear from her who it could be. She then introduced her companion to me by her first name Elfriede, as was customary.

She was a Roman Catholic nun. She lived in a convent in Amstetten in the province of Lower Austria. She regularly visited Vienna from there for periodic medical checkups of her eyesight at the eye clinic. When she heard about me and my destiny from the deputy senior eye specialist during one of her visits, she compassionately volunteered to help me spiritually. I was deeply moved by her generous support and the comfort she gave me at this crucial juncture in my life.

Whenever the nun came to the hospital for her eyesight medical check-up, she automatically visited me in my ward. She would walk me out to a quiet place in the garden of the hospital where she would teach me how to play the guitar. She taught me to sing children's song lyrics as a way to facilitate my acquisition of the German language.

I was so pleased when she gave the guitar to me as a present. She had actually brought it with her all the way from her convent in Amstetten. I was so grateful for her dedication because, all of a sudden, the gaps between her visits to the hospital began to be shorter. She was visiting me almost once every week, teaching me the guitar and songs, and practicing mobility skills with me all the time.

I had just finished having my breakfast one late morning in the first week of September 1969 when my social counsellor arrived to see me, accompanied by a gentleman Hans Polster from the Austrian National Red Cross. He was the officer responsible for the welfare and medical treatment of the wounded Biafran soldiers who were now in the country as guests of the people.

Actually, the gentleman told me that he had served in the Austrian military force before joining the Austrian National Red Cross. Therefore, he understood the physical and psychological problems I was facing at the moment. He was friendly and very kind to me, and executed his responsibilities over me in a highly professional manner all the time.

Like my social counsellor, the gentleman was like an older brother to me. Even when he became the secretary general of the Austrian National Red Cross in the following year, he never wavered or ceased his compassion and commitment to me and my welfare. He stood firmly by me, always ready to give me a helping hand and encouragement, until I succeeded at last.

As my social counsellor and the Austrian National Red Cross official stood beside my bed, they greeted me in a friendly manner and enquired about my well-being. Then my social counsellor reminded me that it was the beginning of September when all schools in the eastern province of Austria re-opened. They had come to move me from the hospital to a designated home for the blind in the city. From there, I would be attending the Federal Institute for the Blind, located in the second district of Vienna.

While I packed up my clothes and other belongings into my portmanteau, including my guitar from the Roman Catholic nun, they walked over to the personnel office of the hospital to settle all administrative matters concerning me. I went round to salute my immediate neighbours in the ward. The 'papa' was very sad that I was leaving. He said that he would miss me a great deal, but wished me well in all my endeavours.

When we arrived at the Red Cross car in the parking lot of the hospital, my social counsellor assisted me to my seat in the back of the car while the Austrian National Red Cross official carried my luggage, including my guitar into the boot. Then they sat in the front, with the Red Cross official driving. We chatted, joked, and laughed together all the way. I was in such good spirits.

It was a relatively long journey with a lot of traffic on the way as we drove on through the city. We finally arrived at our destination—the Home for the Blind (*Blindenheim*) at number 80 Josefstädterstraße in the eighth district of the city of Vienna.

I was terribly excited as we waited at the gate for someone to let us into the building. It took a while before the janitor arrived and opened the gate for us. He recognized my social counsellor and the Red Cross official because they had been there several times for administrative and logistical matters on my behalf. They briefly exchanged a few words with one another in German, which I barely comprehended.

We walked through the huge courtyard, with the Red Cross official carrying my luggage and my social counsellor carrying my guitar. Behind us now was the section of the building that housed the personnel offices of the administration and the arrival hall from the entrance gate. On our right and in front of us was a large garden with thick bushes and hedges; beautiful flowerbeds; and big, high trees. There were benches around for sitting and relaxing.

The building was an old monastery that had once housed Roman Catholic monks. But when it was abandoned as a monastery, a wealthy Austrian benefactor purchased it and generously made it available to blind people as their own home in Vienna. A section of the garden had once been used as a cemetery. One could still read from the gravestones the names of some of the monks who were buried there.

As we continued walking along the path of the courtyard, on our left hand side was a huge building in which the blind residents lived. The building was not excessively tall. It had only three floors. On the ground floor were the kitchen, the dining hall, and other rooms for recreational activities. The blind residents were all housed on the first and second floors of the building.

We entered the building through a large door and walked straight to the staircase. After climbing a flight of stairs, we arrived on the first floor of the building. As we walked along an elaborate and a relatively long corridor, I observed that the doors to the rooms were on the one side, and on the other side was an empty high wall.

When we finally arrived at the right door, we entered my room. My social counsellor and the Red Cross official showed me around the room and helped me to unpack my belongings. It was the first of two large rooms that had been joined together.

There were two blind residents in each room. The residents of the second room passed through ours to go into their own room. Each of us had in our corner a bed, a wardrobe, a table for reading and writing, and some extra space for other limited activities. There were only male residents on my floor. The female residents were housed on the upper floor.

After showing me around, the Red Cross official jokingly commented that the room was like that of a first-class hotel. I was not surprised at the comparison because my 'home' in the geriatric ward of the hospital was no match to my new home in any way.

I settled down quickly in my new home. The residents were very friendly. There were many young people of my age among them. But the majority of the residents were older people. Unlike the older residents at the hospital in Lainz, however, they were not limited to their beds. They were physically fit to go for walks in the garden or around the walls of the building, or even out in the city.

There was a healthy atmosphere of genuine comradeship among the residents of the blind home. We saw each other as peers. I was constantly benefiting from their long-standing experience in living as blind people. It was a very crucial time for me, since I had actually no experience whatsoever living as a blind person. I knew that I would continue to discover more of the power of the mind's eye through these peers.

Some of the young residents who had occupations went to work for different enterprises in the city. Others like me went to the Federal Institute for the Blind to acquire vocational and rehabilitation training. The rest of the residents were on disability pensions, based on their visual impairment.

I was extremely fortunate to have been given some tutoring and mobility training while I was in the hospital in Lainz. The training proved to be a big bonus to me in coping with the journey from the home for the blind to the Federal Institute for the Blind. I was one of four residents who travelled daily from there to the institute.

Every morning, once we were out of the gate of the home for the blind, passers-by guided us to the train station in the Josefstädterstrasse, from whence we travelled by the city train (Stadtbahn) to the Schottenring train station and continued by bus to Wittelsbachstraße in the second district of Vienna. Then we walked our way through to the institute at number 5 Wittelsbachstraße.

I was now used to strangers on the street taking my arm and guiding me to my desired destination. This had been one of my major concerns and fears at the onset of my blindness. I could not imagine that individuals, who were totally strangers to me, would be willing to sacrifice their time and energy to guide me to any destination. I was, therefore, stunned that this was possible in the society in which I now lived. People around me, even strangers on the streets, generously offered their support to me wherever I wanted to go.

Before I knew it, I was already comparing the society I had come from with the one I was presently living in. In my homeland, when I had my sight, I did not see blind people living respectable lives in the society. They never interacted freely with the other citizens. They looked pitiable and wretched. They simply sat lamentably at road junctions or were escorted by little children begging for food or money every day from dawn to dusk. I swore to myself that I would not live that kind of life.

The prophetic words of the deputy senior eye specialist at the eye clinic in the hospital in Lainz were dawning on me. I was beginning to sense a society that cared for its members. There were plenty of opportunities for all individuals to excel in it. I assured myself quietly that, like other members of society, I must grab this opportunity and make the best out of it.

These were the kinds of opportunities I had ceaselessly longed for in my adolescence, but that had been denied me due to circumstances beyond my control. Thanks goodness they had now returned to me in the twilight of blindness in a foreign country!

At the Federal Institute for the Blind, there were two distinct groups of students. In the first group were students from the ages six to nineteen years. These students were mainly congenitally blind, or were developing visual impairment in their adolescence. In the second group were adult students. They were mainly adventitiously blind, or were developing visual impairment in their adulthood. They were men and women of working age.

Some of them had lost their previous jobs because of their visual impairment. Others were hoping to enter the job market in the sighted world. They had all come to the institute to acquire the skills that would improve opportunities for them on the job market. Some strove to regain their lost jobs. I belonged to this second group of students.

I observed right from the outset that rehabilitation and occupational training were to be the focus of my education. I was taught the basics of mobility and daily living skills, as well as how to read and write in the Braille system. For my prospective occupation, I was trained to work as a telephone operator on a telephone switchboard in an industrial environment.

The atmosphere at the institute helped me immensely and facilitated my rehabilitation. I was surrounded by people of all ages. The teachers were highly professional in their work, and had full understanding of my exceptional circumstances, especially that I had come from a totally different culture. They were very supportive of me, and, as I constantly noticed, were determined to see that I succeeded in my ambition.

What a friendly environment! Many of the students talked to me, and some even desired to touch and feel my hair, which I always happily granted to them. Many of them had not seen or touched and felt the hair of a Black African before. They were always excited to be around me. My unlimited interaction with them contributed greatly to the speed with which I could easily master the German language.

I expanded the things I learned at the institute to discover more of the power of the mind. As I now realized, the power of the mind was nothing more than my applying conscientiously the faculties of my other remaining senses to perceive, appreciate, and love the fullness of nature and my surroundings. These were my senses to hear, to smell, to feel, and to taste.

I was highly impressed at the speed with which the younger students were clattering on their Braille typewriters, flying their fingers over the Braille texts, and reading aloud fluently. They were so proficient in the system that their speed of writing and reading could be comparable to that of sighted people. They had learned to read and write in the Braille system right from their childhood.

As I listened to them in action, I wondered if I would be able to achieve that level of proficiency one day. But I was not alone in this situation. The other older students, who had not learned to read and write in Braille from their childhood, were also struggling to master it. To understand the Braille system and to master it were two different abilities. One could understand the system in about thirty minutes of coaching. But to be proficient in it required a long time of practice and patience, as well as exceptional sensitivity in the fingertips.

But I was most grateful to Louis Braille, who invented the system, for my ability to read and write again. My initial fears that I might not be able to do so at the onset of blindness were now totally abated. I could now write and read any text by myself, such as essays, mathematics, letters, and numbers. I could now write and read in any language I desired to learn—like German. What a big joy!

So I was fascinated by the life history of Louis Braille and the circumstances surrounding his invention of the Braille system. *He was also a blind fellow like me*, I said to myself. If he were alive today and living in our country, he might be here at the institute, either as a teacher or a fellow student.

Now, at the Federal Institute for the Blind here in Vienna, Austria, I could confirm what the deputy senior eye specialist had told me that evening at my bedside at the hospital in Lainz. The Braille system was a method that was widely used by blind people to read and write. It was developed in 1821 by Louis Braille.

I practiced very hard to feel and master the positions of the dots in the Braille cells. Each Braille cell has six dot positions, arranged in two vertical columns of three dots each. The dots in the cell are universally numbered 1, 2, and 3 from top to bottom of the left hand column, and 4, 5, and 6 from top to bottom of the right hand column. I found it to be a very clever system, because with the six dots in various combinations of raised and un-raised positions, it is possible to form sixty-four permutations, which exceeds the twenty-six letters of the alphabet and the umlauts of most languages. The horizontal lines of Braille text are separated by a space, as is printed text, making it possible to differentiate the dots of one line from the Braille text above and below. The punctuation and number signs are represented by their own unique set of characters.

I found our lessons in touch typewriting much easier than the other students at the institute. My previous experience proved to be a big asset to me. I had practiced the technique for a year when I attended the Inyamah's Commercial Institute at Aba, Nigeria, in 1961. So I concentrated more on mastering the German keyboard layout and improving my proficiency.

But the Braille shorthand typing lessons were trickier. We were drilled in taking shorthand dictations in Braille and typing the texts out on the normal typewriter. The Braille machine was quite small. We typed the Braille texts on a long strip of paper that was wound into a roll, which we inserted into the Braille machine. The roll of paper unwound as we typed text onto it through the keyboard.

But I especially enjoyed the theoretical part of our lessons in telephony because of my previous studies of electricity and magnetism. I was already familiar with the invention of the telephone and the developments in telecommunications. So I was able to follow the lessons very easily without much difficulty, even with the present level of my German comprehension.

The practical part of the lessons was extremely daunting. As we were deemed prospective telephone operators, we had to learn to remember at random 1000 names and their associated telephone extensions.

The drilling was necessary because, out there in the real world, the many companies (large or small) had telephone systems that connected numerous staff members, each of whom had a separate number. The visually impaired telephone operator was expected to handle all telephone enquiries immediately from the switchboard without having to obtain the information first from the telephone directory.

The exact title of our profession was 'enterprise telephonist'. It was one of the high-profile occupations for the visually impaired at the time. Initially, the switchboard was technically modified so that a visually impaired telephonist could work on it. The light indicators on the switchboard were modified with vibrating needles that the visually impaired telephonist could feel when calls came in.

But, as we were being trained, a new piece of adaptive technology came out on the market. It was the Siemens Ring. This was a smart device, which was worn on the finger and held over the light indicators on the switchboard. It converted the vibrations of the needles into sounds, which were simultaneously intercepted by the blind telephonist.

Thus, the visually impaired telephonist was able to be in full control of the switchboard. For us blind telephonists at the time, the invention of the Siemens Ring was as miraculous as the landing on the moon. We freely joked about it, because, incidentally, it had been only a few months earlier, in June 1969, that the first human being landed on the moon.

I must confess that commuting daily by public transport between the blind home and the institute placed me squarely in the hub of my host society. I was able to experience at first hand its stark difference from my native society. It was a completely different culture and setup. I naturally noticed the difference in language first, but the food, the music, and other aspects of the culture were different, as were the weather and clothing.

All the people around me were friendly and open to me, and I listened zealously to their speech and followed diligently the movements of their tongues and lips when they spoke to me. I was not timid to ask them questions and gladly accepted their corrections of my German. I was extremely ambitious in learning the language.

I was not at all particular about my food. I had a good appetite not only for the delicious Viennese cuisine but also for all the foods of the people. I especially enjoyed eating the apple strudel (*apfelstudel*) and spaghetti.

One Sunday evening, I walked across the road from the blind home to a restaurant. The waiter gave me a friendly welcome and assisted me to a dining table. Thereafter, he asked me, 'Sir, what would you like to drink?' I said, 'A mug of beer, please.' He quickly brought me a mug of beer and left me to attend to the other guests.

After a while, he came back and asked me, 'Sir, what would you like to eat?' Without wasting any time because I knew exactly what I wanted, I said, '*Einmal Schuhpasta.*' The waiter became suddenly silent. I wondered what might have gone wrong, because he was still standing there, which indicated he had not taken my order correctly.

I could sense that his attention was intensely focused on me. Then, he politely replied to me in astonishment, 'But we don't serve something like that here for people to eat. Tomorrow is Monday. You can probably purchase it from the shop in the next house.' I repeated my order exactly as before and insisted that it was what I desired to eat for the evening.

The waiter paused and quietly departed from me. After a while, he returned with something on a small plate and asked me to taste it. I took a bit of it with the fork and tasted it as the waiter had suggested. I recognized it immediately and said to the waiter, 'Yes, this is exactly what I want to eat.' The waiter laughed loudly and said, 'No, it is not Schuhpasta but Pastachutta. I was very embarrassed when the waiter patiently explained to me that *Schuhpasta* actually means *shoe paste*. The Viennese habitually also said Pastachutta to spaghetti. Notwithstanding, I did enjoy eating the real spaghetti with an exceptional appetite when the waiter finally brought it to me.

The mistake was undeniably my eagerness of listening at the people's mouths when they spoke to me. In the dining rooms at the institute and in the blind home, my fellow peers identified spaghetti exactly the way I had said it to the waiter in the restaurant. But I had learned to pronounce it in the typical and original Viennese dialect.

Whilst I was very pleased with the overwhelming reception given to me by the people around me, I did not find the weather particularly friendly all the time. In May 1969, as we first arrived in the country, the weather was extremely friendly and it continued like that until a few months later.

When I was in Africa, I had heard about the various seasons of the year and the climate in Europe, but, of course, I had never had the opportunity to experience them in reality. But the Roman Catholic nun explained them nicely to me through one of the children's songs she taught me. The song was about a mother who had four children. They were Winter, Spring, Summer, and Autumn. Spring brought the flowers. Summer brought the clovers. Autumn brought the grapes. Winter brought the snow.

Of the four children, three had come and gone, and would come back next year. They were all invariably friendly to me. But we were presently in the middle of Winter, which was the fourth child of that mother. It was cold and freezing. It was a big shock to me because I had never experienced anything of the kind in my life.

I came from a climate zone where the temperatures could be above plus 60 degrees Celsius. I could not imagine surviving in temperatures below zero degrees Celsius. But, whether I liked it or not, I was presently in that situation. My social counsellor tried to explain to me that winter could also be as friendly as the other seasons. All I needed was to be appropriately dressed for the weather.

But no matter how many layers of underwear, trousers, and pullovers I put on, I never felt warm. The senior sister of my social counsellor knitted an especially warm woollen muffler and sweater for me, which I wore over the other layers of warm clothing. I then wore a pair of furred leather gloves, heavy furred winter boots, winter trousers, and a heavy furred winter coat and a thick woollen Siberian hat, which covered my ears and face. But, at least I did not need my eyes to see!

I felt so uncomfortable in such attire. And I felt I must look like one of the astronauts who had landed on the moon a few months earlier. But as my social counsellor explained to me, winter could be equally pleasing if one was adequately dressed. I realized that I could not be running around Vienna in T-shirts and sandals in all seasons as I did in my little village in the tropics.

It had been snowing for days in December, and it was

Christmastime. I had never seen or touched the snow in reality. I had only seen it in films and as layers of ice in the refrigerator at one of my uncles' house in Nigeria.

Since our arrival in the country in May, people had been talking to me about winter and the snow. I had been excited and curious when winter finally arrived and the snow began to fall. The snow whitened everything outside the house— the cars, trees, grass, roads, and buildings.

I was greatly amused when I continuously felt the flakes of snow, which were blown around in the air by the wind before they fell on my face and clothing. I felt all the things I touched with my fingers outside the home unbearably chilly and cold, as they were covered with snow. But I could not be restrained in any way by my curiosity in touching and feeling the snow. It was a strange feeling as the cold penetrated mercilessly right through my skin, body, and bones.

I had never celebrated Christmas in this kind of climatic condition. There was a stark contrast in the way Christmas was celebrated in these climatic conditions. In my little village in Nigeria, Christmas festivities were outdoor events. But I totally understood that it could not be celebrated like that here, given the predominance of the cold winter season.

As the evening of 24 December was fast approaching, I could physically feel and smell the spirit of Christmas in the air. All the shops and public buildings were festooned with Christmas decorations. In our blind home, the dining hall, the clubroom, and the trees in the garden were all beautifully decorated in Christmas motif. Men, women, and children were out in the shops purchasing presents. It was a very hectic and stressful period for everyone, I observed.

As in all schools in the country, we were on vacation at the Federal Institute for the Blind. Our vacation lasted until the second week of January in the New Year. Throughout that period, I was invited by many of my Austrian friends to their homes for Christmas. It was a joyous and solemn occasion, which they all wanted me to celebrate with them. I was especially happy because it was my very first Christmas experience in the country. It was also the first Christmas festivity in many years that I was able to celebrate in a quiet and peaceful atmosphere. I was not afraid of bombs and explosions from the Nigerian warplanes and their artillery gunfire.

One of my Viennese friends invited me to his home on Christmas Eve. When I arrived in their home, the children and their father were busy in the sitting room decorating the Christmas tree. They hung candles, a variety of cookies, little bells, and angels on all the branches of the tree. Then they placed all their presents, which had been colourfully wrapped, under the tree. When they finished, the Christmas tree was so beautiful, and the air in the room was filled with the nice smell of the tree and the cookies. I had never experienced anything like that before in my life.

My hosts told me that the evening of 24 December was the climax of the traditional Christmas festivity in the country. The celebrations began with a reading from the Holy Bible. We all sat around the table and listened as my friend read from the scriptures the story on the birth of Jesus Christ as narrated by one of the Gospels. Then we sang together some of the traditional Christmas songs, like *Stille Nacht, heilige Nacht* ('Silent Night, Holy Night').

Subsequently, one of the children distributed the presents to their rightful owners according to the names written on the parcels. It was an exceedingly happy moment, full of excitement as each member of the family received and opened his or her own parcel. I was also given some presents, like chocolates, cookies, and winter clothing—sweaters, pullovers, and woollen gloves, hat, and muffler.

I could not stop admiring the society in which I presently

lived and the people around me. At the beginning, I thought it was love at first sight. But the longer I lived here, the more I discovered the strength of the people through the power of the mind's eye. They were what I called, 'practical-thinking' stock. I tried to clarify this qualification by comparing my host society with the one I originated from. If we dug a well in the village, we drew our water from it with our bucket tied to a long rope. We accepted this process as the end of the road, and continued drawing our water from the well like that for ages without considering other solutions.

If my host society were in a similar situation, this process would not be acceptable for the long haul. Someone would think of a way to simplify the process and would perhaps come up with the Archimedes principle. A wooden pole might be mounted close to the well, with a long stick nailed to it like a cross. With the bucket tied to one end of the stick, only minimal force would have to be applied on the other end of the stick to let the bucket down to the bottom of the well, fill it with water and draw it up to the surface.

I compared the functioning of my host society to the way in which the little ants organized themselves. I called it the 'ants' mentality'. When I had my vision, I watched millions of little ants in my village as they laboured very hard to build their pyramids. They walked unimaginable distances to find food and retrieve the raw materials for constructing their pyramids. With their superb and meticulous organization, discipline, and hard labour, these little ants were able to build huge pyramids and develop excellent and thriving communities of great size and strength. Without doubt, development, or the lack of it, depended on the willingness of the brain and the mind to appreciate the advantages and disadvantages for the survival of the species in nature.

The secret of development lay squarely in the good organizational skills of the species that had embraced it.

Human development did not come before money and luxury. Development came first, then money and luxury. It was the impression I had of my host society, one of whose integral members I was becoming gradually by default.

One of the skills I learned at the Federal Institute for the Blind was using the white cane as a basic instrument for my independent mobility. Actually, I had discovered that the cane provided me a unique method of identifying my special needs among my sighted counterparts when I was travelling. It strengthened my ability to perceive and interpret correctly the ambient cues. As a powerful 'feeler' attached to my hand, it widened my sphere of perception, and thereby provided me an enormous feeling of security.

The longer I used the white cane, the more I discovered its inevitable powers in my ability to overcome the limitations of blindness. Whenever I went out walking on my own, all I needed was to take up my white cane and put it in to service.

While I tapped along the road in my journeys with the white cane, I received first-hand information about the texture of the ground and the nature of the objects around me. I was amazed to discover that the sensitivity in my fingers was automatically extended to the white cane, and the time span I required to process the information I perceived was extremely minimal.

Frankly speaking, the white cane was crucial in my ability to make the best use of my other senses. If I was searching for the entrance to a coffee house while walking along the pavement, I focused my nose on the odours coming out of the various buildings on my way.

Once I smelled the coffee, I tapped my white cane at any hard object, like the pavement. Then I applied my sense of hearing and listened to the sound that was echoed back to me. I easily found the entrance to the coffee house, as I skilfully followed the direction of the echo. Sometimes, I snapped my fingers to produce the same effect.

The white cane enabled me to walk in a straight line, keeping my direction and orientation always secured. I still use this skill today to find my way to some of the popular shops in the city for my needs of textiles, shoes, perfumes, flowers, groceries, and even to find apothecaries, restaurants, food kiosks, and many more.

The longer I was blind, the more I discovered that the power of my mind's eye was more than I could imagine. When I was sighted, I did not realize that I was constantly utilizing my visual ability in combination with my mind's eye to organize the nature around me. I thought I was only using my visual ability to identify and recognize all the things in my immediate and distant environment. But now, without my vision, I discovered that I automatically identified and recognized organic and nonorganic things, animate and inanimate objects, by using imaginary 'markers'. These imaginary markers were available to me in two forms. One form, I called 'virtual markers' and the other form, I called 'enhanced virtual markers'.

If I spoke to someone on the phone, or met an individual in a room or in the street, I applied the virtual markers to identify and recognize that person on my own. Some of these virtual markers included the voice of the individual; his or her body movement; style of talking, laughing, and smiling; the smell of his or her body and clothing.

The image of the person or object was represented and stored in my knowledge bank as I imagined it. I widened my imagination of the image of the person or the object with enhanced virtual markers. These were the additional descriptions given to me about the person or the object by someone else, or facts that I learned if I was permitted to physically touch and feel the person or object by myself.

The image I created in this way was solely for my own perception for identifying the person or the object, and I never shared it with anyone else. People often asked me to feel their faces and tell them how they looked to me. I always declined to indulge in such an embarrassing exercise, because the image I would make of them, based on the application of my imaginary markers, might not match exactly the reality of their appearance.

As an adventitiously blind person, I could compare and relate my experiences to the sighted world with my skilful utilization of the imaginary markers. On the other hand, if I were congenitally blind, I wondered how I would do it. Perhaps, the imaginary markers would still have adequate meaning and applications for me, but in a different manner.

I found great inspiration in my education at the Federal Institute for the Blind in Vienna. It proved to be the bedrock for my future aspirations. I learned quite a lot from my teachers and my fellow blind students as I prepared to meet the challenges ahead of me. My interactions with them at different levels and at all times motivated me not to surrender to blindness but to confront it stubbornly. I also learned that it was left to me to grab the opportunities available to me and to make the best use of them.

My education at the institute concluded naturally in June 1970 at the end of the school year. I had completed my education in rehabilitation and occupational skills very successfully. I was fully trained as an enterprise telephonist, meaning that I was competent to work on any telephone switchboard of any large or small enterprise.

At the institute, it was customary to hold a special ceremony for the award of the certificates to the students at the end of their education. On the day of our own passing out ceremony, we were called up, one after the other, to receive our certificates from the director of the institute.

It was a unique and very solemn occasion, because all the students and teachers of the institute gathered in the festivity hall for the ceremony. When my name was called out, I proudly walked up to the director and received my certificate from him. He shook my hand, congratulated me for my achievement, and wished me many successes in my future career as a telephonist.

But I did not want to settle for an easy life. Both at the Federal Institute for the Blind and in the blind home, I had heard people talking about an evening secondary school for adults. The more I heard about it, the more interested I became. I remembered that it had been my ambition to attend a secondary school when I finished the primary school in Nigeria. But I could not do so because my father lacked the financial means to support me.

I told my social counsellor that I would like to attend an evening secondary school for adults to get a diploma, if possible. Such a school was located at Henriettenplatz number 6 in the 15th district of the City of Vienna. It was the Federal Grammar School for Working People (*Bundesrealgymnasium für Berufstätige*). The classes were held in the evenings for working people who wanted to study for their high school diploma (*Matura*).

My counsellor listened thoughtfully and professionally as I explained the reasons why I intended to pursue that kind of education at this stage. We discussed my intentions thoroughly over several days. She understood my ambitions and was receptive to them, as she was by now fully familiar with my past history.

But, as she told me, she had a hard time selling the idea to her superiors in the Social Welfare Department of the Municipality of the city of Vienna. They raised many questions to support their scepticism: What will he do as a blind person with a secondary school diploma? They argued that the evening secondary school education would cost them a great deal of money.

They wondered how I would get the required textbooks because almost none of them was available in Braille or recorded format. As I had been scarcely only one year in the country, they also questioned whether my proficiency in the German language was sufficient to permit me to participate in the classroom activities.

They told her that only a negligible number of blind people had managed to attend a secondary school and the university to date in the country. There was almost no hope of employment opportunity for a blind academic on the job market.

Even the teachers at the Federal Institute for the Blind were disappointed when they heard that I was not going to practice the telephonist profession for which they had trained me. The institute had established relations with a network of collaborative enterprises who could employ their blind telephonists.

These teachers expressed similar pessimism to the colleagues of my social counsellor. Other blind persons at the institute and in the blind home were equally sceptical. Their overall attitude was, 'Let's wait and see'.

But my social counsellor succeeded at last in selling the idea to her department, with the only condition that the school must agree to admit me. The Social Welfare of the Municipality of the City of Vienna would fully sponsor my education.

My social counsellor accompanied me to the school to meet the director. At the beginning of our conversation, he sounded somewhat sceptical. He raised a couple of questions that sounded similar in substance to those raised by the Social Welfare Department.

But my social counsellor told him that I would be attending a German course for foreigners at the Vienna University during the day, since I would not be at work like his other students. At the end of our conversation, the director agreed to admit me to the school, but for a trial, as he put it.

In September 1970 when the school opened, I earnestly began my secondary school education at the Federal Grammar School for Working People. I did not have to make much preparation for it. I had a desktop reel-to-reel tape recorder with a sufficient number of empty tapes, a Brailling machine, Braille plate and a stylus, a bunch of carbon papers, packets of blank sheets of writing paper, and an abacus. But the most important of all the tools at my disposal was my talented brain.

The school provided different fields of specialization, which granted the diploma (*Reifeprüfung* or *Matura*) that was needed for the student to study at the university. Our lessons focused on general education in the humanities, science, and languages.

I mobilized squads of supporters within and without the school. I was now very confident with my mobility outdoors. My skills were sufficiently developed that I could travel independently. I went to school every evening by tram and returned by the city train (*Stadtbahn*). I carried in my schoolbag the only classroom working tools that were available to me.

My classmates were extremely friendly to me. They supported me generously. I was the only foreigner in the class and the only visually impaired person. They were all adults, and of my age. We were like members of a harmonious family. It was not surprising, because we understood fairly well that we were in the same boat and pursuing a similar goal.

We also understood that, in order to attain our desired goals, we must work conscientiously and hard. An atmosphere of collaboration prevailed in our classroom throughout the years of our study. I was an indisputable rallying point for my classmates. Whilst supporting me with sighted tasks, they equally drew their motivation from me to meet the challenges of the classroom culture.

Whenever I arrived in the classroom, I distributed carbon papers and blank sheets of writing paper to my colleagues. They used them to produce copies of their notes and scripts for me, so I could have copies of whatever the teacher had dictated or written on the blackboard.

They took turns in this undertaking, which they distributed among themselves according to the lessons, making certain that the scripts were legibly written. At the end of each lesson, I collected the copies of the scripts to take home with me.

In the blind home, my volunteer helpers visited me regularly to read and explain (when necessary) the contents of the scripts, which I recorded on the desktop reel-to-reel tape recorder. It was an extremely time-consuming task because our studies covered over thirteen subjects, ranging from mathematics to natural sciences and philosophy.

My social counsellor had spread the word about the urgency of my study needs at various quarters in the city. Different groups of young people reacted positively to her appeal for voluntary assistance to me. Students from the Association of Young Catholics and from the Austrian Young Red Cross came to read for me in the blind home voluntarily. They came to help me as members of their individual organization or even on their own. They came to me during the day and at weekends.

Sometimes, some of these young people accompanied

me to my school in the evening. They took me out with them occasionally and included me in their group's recreational activities in the city or in the provinces. They were all young people like me, and they perfectly understood my desires and aspirations.

One of them was Renate Schneider, whom I had met at the evening grammar school where we were both students. She lived with her parents Wilhelm and Ernestine in the 16th district of the city. Her brother Willy and his wife Christine lived in the same house with their two children, Martin and Lissy Renate and I became close friends, and married in 1975.

My social counsellor was professionally correct in her judgement that I should mingle with young people of my age. It made a huge difference in my life. I was genuinely motivated by these people that I did not have the time anymore to occupy myself with the negativity of blindness on my life.

I went out with some of them to social parties, football matches, and discotheques. We sang gospel songs and played the guitar together. Incidentally, the 1968 students' riots in Paris were still having its aftermath effect on young people of the age, and we were at the height of the worldwide protests against the war in Vietnam.

Very often, I dressed up in hippie attire like my young friends and we went out to perambulate in the *Volksgarten* (public park).

The support I got from these young people was especially indispensable to me for my studies at the evening grammar school and for my German language course for foreigners at the University of Vienna. It was easy for them to read and decipher the handwritten scripts of my classmates, as they were familiar with our lessons in biography, geography, chemistry, ancient and modern history, physics, mathematics,

Latin, German, English, philosophy, religion, music, and arts.

I relied mainly on the abilities of my brain to take part in our classroom activities. I particularly enjoyed assignments in mathematics at home and at the school. All my teachers were exceptionally cooperative in their support for me in the classroom.

Our maths teacher was always amazed at the speed with which I could mentally calculate the results of the maths assignments she had written on the blackboard. To help me follow the lessons, she habitually read out the assignment as she wrote it on the blackboard for the other students.

I would concentrate deeply, calculating simultaneously as I listened to her announcements. I would use the abacus to keep track of larger numbers. Then I would immediately have the result ready long before the other students could do so. I had the advantage because I had always been strong in mathematics since my primary school days in Nigeria.

Whenever I had maths exam, I brought my Brailling machine with me to the classroom. I did all the calculations on the machine in combination with the abacus and my mental ability. But for the exams in other subjects, such as Latin, English, and German, I typed my answers directly onto my portable typewriter, which I also brought with me to the classroom from home. But it was extremely difficult for me to correct any mistakes.

I profited a great deal from the vocabulary mastery drill in our Latin lessons. My German vocabulary expanded as I learned the Latin words and their varying meanings in German. The Latin reading textbook we used was *Liber Latinus*. I was extremely lucky to have it in Braille. Some blind fellow, who had studied Latin long before me, had had it translated manually into Braille at the Federal Institute for the Blind. It was the only available copy, and I made sure that it remained in solidly usable condition for another blind fellow who might require it in the future.

But for the literary works by renowned Latin writers, such as Cato, Aurelius, Virgil, Plautus, Ovid, and Julius Caesar, I obtained the textbooks from the libraries for the blind in Eastern and Western Germany.

For my studies in geography, I used a Braille atlas of the globe. The atlas consisted of thirty-five relief cards, with illustrations of the political and physical maps of the globe. The tactile illustrations of the landscapes, oceans, rivers, mountains, cities, and country boundaries, and so on, were represented by abbreviations. The atlas was accompanied by a register in which the abbreviations were explained in detail. The dimension of each relief card was about twenty inches by twenty inches.

The education standard of our school was extremely high in comparison to that in other countries. I was so fortunate to have been educated there. I noticed that we were taught things in the school that students in other countries only began to learn at the university level. For example, our curricula included philosophy, which was not common in other countries at the grammar school level.

We were introduced to psychology, psychoanalysis, and behaviourism, basics of logic and contemporary political theories such as, Titoism, Maoism and the like. I found the knowledge especially interesting because we were at the height of the cold war and the fight for supremacy by the two major economic and political systems of the world, which were capitalism and planned economy.

My sponsors, the Social Welfare department of the Municipality of the city of Vienna and the Austrian National Red Cross, understood very well how to make me feel at home in the country. Every summer, during the school vacations, they sponsored recreational holidays for me outside the city.

In the summers of 1971 and 1972, I participated in the International Red Cross Camp for young people. It was hosted annually by the Austrian National Red Cross in the Wine Production School in Langenlois in the District of Krems in the Province of Lower Austria. Organizations of the Red Cross from other countries sent their young members to participate in the camp.

In the years I participated in the activities of the camp, young people from England, Scotland, Finland, Norway, Denmark, Switzerland, Czechoslovakia, Sweden, and West Germany participated in the camp as members of their country's delegation. I was the only disabled/blind participant from the African continent.

I enjoyed very much my holidays in the camp. We undertook different activities inside and outside the camp together. One of our common regular recreational activities was the early morning physical exercise, which I led enthusiastically. I was always in the middle of the circle, stretching and jumping in front of them. I encouraged the young boys and girls to exercise with me as we used to do in the military. It was a memorable occasion for me as I experienced these young people jumping, running, stretching, and laughing together with me. At times, many of them could not endure the exercises for too long, as I kept firing them up to continue. They joked about my harsh style of encouragement and nicknamed me '"the slave driver'.

Our indoor activities included folk songs and dances. Each delegation taught their music to the others, and we all shared in the activities. Some of our outdoor activities included visits to an old peoples' home to entertain the residents. We also went out to clean up the nearby beaches.

We hand picked the trash that was scattered around the area and abandoned by some thoughtless visitors.

On one occasion, we climbed the Leithagebirge, one of the famous mountains in Lower Austria. Everyone shouted and cheered when I finally arrived on the top of the mountain with my companion. I was one of the very few of the participants in the excursion who could make it to the summit of the mountain. I made many friends among these young people in the camp. My friendship with some of them in Austria and in the other countries has continued until this day.

In December 1972, I changed my living accommodations and moved to the International Students Hostel at number 85 Gymnasiumstraße in the 19th district of the city of Vienna. My social counsellor had convinced her office that it was essential that I should live in an environment that was conducive to my circumstances. The students' hostel was an ideal place for the opportunity. It was much easier for me to obtain help from many young and sighted students living together with me in the hostel. The environment was psychologically and socially more encouraging to me than it had been in the blind home.

My move to the hostel was facilitated by the fact that it belonged to the Municipality of the City of Vienna. The Municipality could easily absorb the costs within its general administrative expenditures. There were several such hostels for students around the city.

When I moved into the hostel, I could confirm the assumptions of my social counsellor. It was one of the most modern hostels in the city, with a complex of high buildings, numbered from A to E. The ground floors of Buildings A, B, and C had large common areas for socializing. The reception area, *mensa* (dining hall), and the administration offices were located on the ground floors of Buildings D and E, respectively.

The layout of the buildings covered a huge area with beautiful hedges, flowers, and bushes. The large lawns between the buildings provided ample opportunities for sports and other recreational activities. It was a beautiful landscape that reminded me of the layout of the campuses for colleges and universities in Nigeria that I had seen such a long time ago.

My boarding room was on the third floor of Building-A. It was self-contained in terms of the practical living needs of a student. I had my bed, a cupboard for clothing, a reading and writing table, a shower, and a washbasin.

Our floor was laid out in a U-shape, with the boarding rooms stretching out in two parallel lines. In the middle stood a long area that housed our kitchen, toilets, and the lift. The layout created two narrow corridors, with the doors to the boarding rooms on one side. At one end of the housing area, opposite the staircase, was the entrance to the lift. At the other end of the housing area was our kitchen. In front of the kitchen, at the base of the U-form, was our common sitting area.

The students were from different countries and continents. A majority of the students were from Austria. My neighbours on both sides were female students. But it had not been always like that. A few months before my arrival at the hostel, male and female students were segregated from one another. The female students were boarded in Buildings C and E, and the male students in Buildings A, B, and D.

The students protested strongly against the segregation policy of the administration, with rallies on the streets, which were supported by the university students' union. The administration ultimately gave in to the demands of the students. The segregation rules were lifted, and the cohabitation of male and female students in the hostel was permitted.

I must confess that the students' hostel was no match to the blind home. It was totally a different environment, which I profoundly appreciated.

I found my travels every evening from the students' hostel to the grammar school very simple. I always had a handful of people to assist me to and from the tram stations.

It was very easy for me to find someone around in the hostel to help me with my classroom work, especially when I was preparing for exams. The students told me that they could refresh their memories of their own days at school when they rehearsed with me.

They were not grammar school students like me. Instead, they were all undergraduates at the university. It was an exception by the administration to admit me to the hostel, as I was not yet studying at the university. The Municipality of the City of Vienna could afford to make such a generous exception on my behalf because it was the rightful owner of the hostel and my benevolent sponsor.

At the beginning of 1975, my secondary education at the Federal Grammar School for Working People came to an end successfully. It had lasted four and a half years (nine semesters) in all. It was, for me, a period of excitement, anxiety, happiness, and a period for pursuing success.

As we had previously completed the required examinations in the various secondary subjects, our final exams at the end were in mathematics, German, Latin, and English. These were our major secondary school diploma subjects. I scored high passing marks in all of them, especially with excellence in mathematics.

Our current and former teachers set the tasks for our written and oral final exams. The board of examiners consisted of our teachers in the respective subjects, the director of our school, and a representative of the Ministry of Education as the chairman.

One of my classmates told me after our oral exam in mathematics that the chairman of the board of the examiners was so taken away by my performance that he pricked up his ears, contracted his ear muscles, and wagged both ears in astonishment. He gave the impression that he could not believe that a visually impaired student could handle and resolve the mathematics tasks mentally in the manner I did. I scored a distinction mark, the highest a student could achieve in mathematics.

On 27 January 1975, at an official ceremony in our school, we received our diplomas, which showed that we had completed our secondary education and were legally entitled to study at the university. It was a solemn and glamorous occasion as we were called up one after the other to received our diplomas directly from the director of our school.

I was exceedingly happy as I walked up to the director and received my own secondary school diploma directly from him. Apart from myself, no one else could tell at that moment how I felt about my achievement so far. The excitement, the happiness, and the secret of that moment remain with me until this day.

When the Social Welfare department of the Municipality of the City of Vienna agreed to sponsor my education at the evening grammar school, the understanding was that, if I qualified from the school, I should continue to study at the university.

But the main challenge for me was to identify what I should study. Originally, my intention was to study something that I could meaningfully practice as a profession if I went back to Nigeria. At first, I considered studying law. But, if I studied law in Austria, it might not be practical for me to practice it professionally in Nigeria. I was told that English law would be a more appropriate subject to study, if I wanted to go back to Nigeria to practice. But any possibility for me to move over to England to study was completely ruled out.

The other option was for me to study mathematics and physics at the University of Vienna. But I quickly ran into a variety of questions with no simple or straightforward answers: How will I have access to the scientific study materials? How will I be able to actively participate in and deliver scientific assignments? How will I be able to practice my profession, either as a teacher or a researcher? The problems I envisaged for such an undertaking seemed insurmountable. Eventually, I dropped the idea of studying mathematics and physics, which would have done justice to my natural talents. I decided to study philology and linguistics in German, English, and French.

I had two choices of direction of study for the profession. I could either study to become a teacher or a researcher. I was convinced that I would be able to practice that kind of profession in Nigeria. I could teach German, English, and French or I could be attached to a university in Nigeria or Austria as a researcher.

At the beginning of the summer semester in March 1975, I enrolled to study philology in German, French, and English at the University of Vienna. I was very proud that my dream to study at a university had been ultimately realized. But at first, I wanted to know more about the history of the Vienna University, which I found very interesting and fascinating. It was founded on March 12, 1365, by Duke Rudolph IV and his brothers Albert III and Leopold III, which is the reason that 'Alma Mater Rudolphina' was added to the name of the university. It was the second oldest university in Central

Europe and the oldest university in the German-speaking world following the Charles University in Prague.

Before I could begin my studies in earnest, I had to overcome certain hurdles that were in my way. I had developed a unique skill for studying at the evening grammar school, which I planned to apply at the university. The devices at my disposal were the desktop reel-to-reel tape recorder, the Brailling machine, the typewriter, the Braille stenograph typewriter, carbon paper, sheets of blank paper, and— a newcomer to my pool of assistive devices—the portable audiocassette recorder. I used it to record the lectures by the professors in the lecture halls. But, before I could do so, I needed to obtain permission from the individual professors. It was very unusual to come into the lecture halls with a tape recorder to record the lectures. It was a scenario with which many professors did not feel comfortable.

I approached the Austrian National Union of Students at the university for support in addressing these unforeseen hurdles. The union was sympathetic and very receptive to my request. It delegated one of its members, who accompanied me to meetings with the individual professors to request permission for me to record the lectures.

We followed this procedure at the beginning of each semester until all the professors became used to my system of work in the lecture halls. It was not surprising that some of the professors were shy on seeing the microphone in front of them. They wanted to make sure that I did not misuse their statements in the lectures. It could happen that the lecturer would digress from the salient topics during the lecture. The digressed statement could be politically or socially sensitive, and the professor concerned would not be happy to have it made public through the news media or otherwise without his or her prior knowledge.

But I assured each and every one of the professors that

I would not misuse the privilege accorded me to record the lectures. I stated that the recordings were only for my personal use in my studies, and not for anyone else. After I had given these assurances to the individual professors, they all felt happy and at ease with me. I did not have any difficulties whatsoever in going into the lecture hall and recording the lectures directly on to my audiocassette tape recorder.

I chose to study for a doctoral degree in philology in German, French, and English. But, before I made that final decision, I consulted fellow students at the counselling section of the office of the Students Union for advice. I also held several discussions on the matter with more experienced students living with me in the students hostel.

The views I exchanged with them in many conversations helped me enormously in finally making my right choice of study. I was convinced that philology provided me the opportunity to understand and widen my knowledge of the literary works and other culturally significant texts of these languages. I pulled up my sleeves and adjusted my method of work to meet my study needs at the university. Without any doubt, these needs were larger and more complex than those I had required at the evening grammar school. I had to read primary literary works in the three languages of my study. I also had to be able to obtain information from the secondary or reference literature of these languages. But I was very fortunate that I could identify reliable sources, especially in the primary literature. I obtained some of these literary works from the Braille libraries in the United Kingdom of Great Britain, the Federal Republic of Germany, the Democratic Republic of Germany, the United States of America, and Austria. I also obtained hundreds of cassettes of recorded literary works from the American Recording Services for the Blind in Paris, France.

The rest of my needs for the reading of printed texts were

fulfilled by my pool of volunteer readers from the students' hostel and at the university. My volunteer readers in the students' hostel extended their help to me by organizing themselves in small groups. They took turns in reading printed materials to me and in accompanying me to and from the university for my lectures.

As I could not take home with me to the hostel the reference materials and the secondary literature works, the University Library Authorities designated a quiet corner in the library reading room to be used by my volunteer readers to read the required information to me. I recorded the readings on my tape recorder. It was a very helpful and practical arrangement, giving me access to the information that was crucial for my research works.

I took my tape recorder with me everywhere in the university, recording all the lectures and similar important information. I usually left the hostel in the mornings and returned in the evenings around eight o'clock, with long hours of taped material in need of processing. I would first have a quick supper and a few hours of sleep. Then I would begin to transfer the information from the tape recorder onto the desktop reel-to-reel tape recorder. It was a tedious task, which on many occasions lasted until the small hours of the morning. I would extract the information I considered most important from the audiocassette recordings and save it on the bigger machine. For example, I might condense a ninety-minute lecture to about ten to fifteens minutes on the bigger machine.

In that process, I ignored and removed all the digressions, the side remarks, the coughs and laughter by the professor and the students alike from the information I transferred to the bigger machine. What I eventually had retained on the bigger machine were the salient points and the thrust of the lectures.

I applied the same strategy of work with the other

information material I had recorded earlier on the audiocassette recorder during the day. I was extremely satisfied with the effectiveness of this method of work, despite the hard work and the stress involved in the process.

With this method of work, I had an excellent opportunity and an exceptional privilege to capture the entire content of any lecture. Sometimes, some of my fellow students consulted me to get the text of a lecture they had been unable to attend, or to correct mistakes in their notes of the lectures.

At the oral exams, the professors were always pleasingly amazed at the correctness of my answers to their questions, which were mostly *ad verbum* to the texts of their lectures. For the written exams, I used the portable typewriter and the Brailling machine to write the exams and other assignments.

As I was studying for a doctoral degree in my chosen faculty, I was required to take a number of mandatory courses in theoretical and practical branches of philosophy. In the practical branch, I was especially interested in the Austrian philosopher Ludwig Wittgenstein and his publication *Tractatus Logico-Philosophicus*. As a matter of fact, the contents of the publication were directly relevant to my field of study. As part of my final examination assignment, I enthusiastically wrote a research paper in which I analyzed Wittgenstein's logics in identifying the relationship between language and reality, as well as defining the limits of science.

In the theoretical branch, I was fascinated by the guiding principle of empiricism 'Nihil est in intellectu quod non antea in senso fuerit' (Nothing in the intellect unless first in the sense) that was developed by Francis Bacon, John Locke, David Hume, and others. John Locke's 'Essay concerning Human Understanding' caused me to reflect on my own ability to acquire knowledge through my perception of the world around me as a blind person.

I wondered constantly how that famous guiding principle of empiricism could be relevant to my situation. Of course, I had acquired significant knowledge of the world around me when I was sighted, from which I was now benefiting a great deal and which I was expanding with the power of the 'mind's eye'. But the thought caused me to reflect on the argument by Leibnitz, who had added '*nisi intellectus ipse*' (except the intellect itself) to the guiding principle of empiricism.

I was highly impressed by Immanuel Kant and his philosophical arguments on epistemology, laid down in his important publications, such as *The Critique of Pure Reason*, in which he investigates the limitations and the structure of reason itself. In his other publication, *The Critique of Practical Reason*, he concentrates his argument on ethics. In *The Critique of Judgment*, he investigates aesthetics and teleology.

Our professor in the theoretical branch of philosophy had the habit of inducing a session for discussions after each lecture. I enjoyed these sessions passionately. On one occasion, we debated Emmanuel Kant's attack on the traditional metaphysics and epistemology and his belief that, with his doctrine of transcendental idealism, he created a compromise between the empiricists and the rationalists.

Kant suggested that metaphysics can be reformed through epistemology, and, by understanding the sources and limits of human knowledge, we asked fruitful metaphysical questions.

In my enthusiasm to impress our professor on the topic, I suggested a geometrical representation of Kant's argument for the metaphysical question. I called the geometrical figure a 'life triangle', represented thus: If we created two points, one of which was the point of birth, including gestation, and the other, the point of death, and drew a straight line to connect the two points, this would represent our 'life span'. If we then drew a line from the point of birth, including gestation, and another line from the point of death. The two lines should meet each other somewhere to construct a triangle.

All metaphysical questions and their answers, if any, would appear within the other parts of the life triangle except the life span line, which described reality. The professor was pleasingly amazed at my contribution to the debates. He welcomed my proposition as another possible way of simplifying Emmanuel Kant's doctrine of transcendental idealism.

Besides these theoretical and practical courses in philosophy, I took courses in linguistics as prescribed by the university administration for my doctoral degree. The courses in introduction to general linguistics were among the most interesting courses I attended at the university. They played a crucial role in framing my mind for the ultimate choice of an academic field for my specialization.

By studying the Indo-Germanic / Indo-European languages, I was equipped with the essential scientific tools for my field research work in linguistics. Even though the lectures were introductory in nature, they were sufficiently holistic to cover recent, ancient, and extinct Indo-European languages.

I admired the work by scholars in their development of the hypothetical proto-language from which all the Indo-European languages descended, including information about their speakers and societies. Comparative linguistics was the essential tool for scholars in their scientific research and ultimate successes.

From a historical perspective, I now clearly understood the linguistic relationship between English, French, and German. That knowledge enabled me to study them together with their history, literature, and culture, grammar, rhetoric, interpretation of authors, and critical traditions with ease.

Our courses in linguistics focused predominantly on contemporary theories and practices. I was mostly attracted to Noam Chomsky's system of generative transformational grammar as outlined in his publication the *Syntactic Structures*. At the beginning, I struggled hard to comprehend this new notion of grammar, but quickly became comfortable with it. According to the new notion of generative transformational grammar, grammar was now understood to cover semantics, phonology, and syntax as an integrated system of rules for relating the pronunciation of a sentence to its meaning. With the new notion in the study of languages, new terminologies emerged, such as phonology, morphology, and phonetics, which had been totally unknown to me before I began studying linguistics.

Each of these terms characterized the study of a unique linguistic feature. For example, phonology is the study of sound patterns within languages. It investigates the sound patterns at a single stage in the development of a language, and identifies which ones could occur and in what position.

Furthermore, morphology investigates the structure and form of words in a language, including inflection, derivation, and the formation of compounds. Phonetics investigates the speech sounds, dealing with their articulation, their acoustic properties, and how they combine to build syllables, words, and sentences. Those were the learning scenario and the building blocks in which our courses in English, French, and German were set.

I never missed a single day of our courses in English linguistics, since I was acquiring so much knowledge from them about the language that I spoke fluently. Even though it was not my mother tongue, I was not foreign to it. I was fascinated by the plethora of events that led to the development of the English language.

Old English was the language spoken by the Anglo Saxons in England. I could now understand the relationships between English and German, which I had wondered about when I first began to learn the German language in my sickbed at the hospital in Lainz some years ago. At that time, I had noticed certain similarities between many words in the two languages, in both their usage and pronunciation.

These courses traced the development of the English language right from its origins to the present day. It originated from continental Europe. According to history, when Britain was under the Roman Empire, the Romans went to the European mainland and recruited soldiers and mercenaries into their occupying army from three Germanic tribes, the Jutes, the Angles, and the Saxons.

At the collapse of the Roman Empire in the fifth century AD, the occupying Roman army retreated from the British Isles. But it was unable to pay off the soldiers and mercenaries it had recruited from the three Germanic tribes into its service. At the end, it paid them off with strips of land on the island nation as compensation.

The Angles were given strips of land in the area of Geordieland in the northeast of England; the Jutes were given strips of land in the Kent area in the south of England; and the Saxons were given strips of land in the Essex area, in the middle of England.

These Germanic tribesmen had brought their language with them over to Britain as it was spoken on the continent. Hence, Old English was also known as Anglo-Saxon English. They quickly established themselves in those areas of Britain where they had been settled by their Roman debtors. They developed dynasties and expanded their sphere of influence on the island.

Actually, I later found out that the story was not as simple as that. It was much more complex than was recounted to us in our linguistic courses. The actual story involved a great many knots and twists amongst the players in the game of history.

But the undeniable truth was that Anglo-Saxon English originated from the German language, based on historical linguistic developments. For instance, Anglo-Saxon English had inflections in its grammar just as German does. It had prefixes and suffixes for words in tenses and declensions.

It was not until in the development of Middle English and the great vowel change of the sixteenth century that these inflections began to be eliminated in the English language. The pronunciation of the umlauts experienced dramatic transition during the great vowel change.

The next changes in the English language occurred in the middle of the nineteenth century. However, the American version of the English language was not affected by these changes. Instead, it retained some of the older characteristics of the English language, such as in the meaning of words and grammar.

In these linguistic courses, we explored the varieties of the English language as they were spoken around the globe. These scholarly conversations prompted me to approach our professor on the variety of English spoken in West Africa. I told him about the variety of the language that was widely spoken in Nigeria. The more I told the professor about it, the more interested he was in it. He became even more excited when I went on to explain to him that I could even speak that Nigerian variety in addition to standard English. I told him that it was called 'pidgin English'.

Of course, the professor had read about various forms of pidgin English, but had never heard it spoken by someone. Pidgin is a simplified but fairly structured form of a language used between two peoples who speak different languages. He asked me to speak my Nigerian pidgin to him. He listened intensely to my narration, but could not make head or tail of my utterances, even though he was a professor of English. It sounded like a foreign language to his ears, although he could vaguely intercept some of the pidgin words and approximate their counterparts in standard English.

We went together through some of the pidgin examples as I spoke them slowly to him. The professor quickly recognized that the pidgin sentences were based on similar principles as the 'guest worker German', which was gradually receiving scholarly attention in contemporary linguistics at the university. The professor remembered that Hugo Schuchardt had carried out a study on such language varieties earlier in the century. It was called 'Lingua Franca' or 'Mischsprachen'. I cautiously asked him if it was all right for me to undertake a similar research work on Nigerian pidgin English in connection with my doctoral degree programme. As I was studying for a doctoral degree in linguistics, I had to write a thesis. I could choose the topic of my thesis from one of the examination subjects in the syllabus of our courses in English. Or, the professor could propose an appropriate topic for me to write about.

The professor happily welcomed my proposal for the field research work on the Nigerian pidgin. In our further discussion, he noted that, until not too long ago, pidgin languages were considered to be peripheral and corrupt in relation to their models. He cited the pioneering work by Hugo Schuchardt on the subject as an example. His theories, and those of other scholars, on the evolution of these languages were subjected to unpopular scientific criticisms and speculations. Many of these criticisms focused on the apparent limited grammar and vocabularies of these languages. I told the professor that these assumptions had provoked my interest in these languages, since the Nigerian pidgin was one of them.

Then the professor paused and spoke softly to me wondering how I would be able to undertake such a study, given my physical disability as a blind scholar. He made it clear to me that such a study involved unavoidable field research work on the spot, which meant travelling to Nigeria and conducting interviews and collecting information material.

But the professor recognized my enthusiasm, ambition, and abilities, which I had proved to him beyond doubt in the various courses. He also calculated the immense benefits to the University of Vienna if I could undertake the research study successfully.

At the end, we agreed that I should undertake the study for my doctoral degree in linguistics as we had discussed. I submitted the final proposal for the study. My study focused on the complex syntactic structures of the Nigerian pidgin, as it had the largest number of speakers in West Africa.

The professor happily approved my proposal, as he considered me to be perfectly suited to undertake such a field research work for the University of Vienna. One of his many reasons for doing so was that it would be much easier for me to obtain the essential data from the informants in Nigeria for the research.

Before I began working on my thesis, I communicated the topic of my thesis and the name of my professor in writing to the dean of academic affairs of the university administration. But my preparations for the field research were based on two approaches. First, I undertook an extensive research on the subject of pidgins and creoles, based on the documents that were available to me at the University of Vienna. (A creole language evolves from a pidgin language and becomes an established language.)

I solicited the assistance of my benevolent army of

volunteer readers to record on audiotape the information which I had extracted from those documents for my scientific analysis. I was able to acquaint myself in this way with sufficient knowledge about the nature and history of pidgins and creoles prior to my field research trip.

The style of my interviews with the informants would be very simple. I chose conversation and narration as the source of my data for the study. In that regard, I would engage the informants in conversations, in which they would be prompted to narrate stories, folklore, and their personal experiences. I prepared a set of questions, which would help me to guide the sessions with the informants.

In the second approach of my preparations for the research trip, I solicited financial, material, and logistical support from various sources. The Austrian Ministry of Science and Research, the Municipality of the City of Vienna, the Austrian National Bank, the Austrian National Red Cross, the Austrian society of the War Blind provided me financial and logistic support.

The phonogrammic archive of the Austrian Academy of Sciences of the University of Vienna provided me technical and material assistance comprised of a superbly high-quality portable tape recorder, a powerful external microphone, and a sufficient number of blank tapes for recording speeches. I was well equipped with state-of-the-art technology, just like a media journalist on a field assignment.

I was extremely excited about my journey to Nigeria in two ways. Not only was I going on a field research trip, but also it would be my first visit to the country in nine years. I had not lived there since the end of the Civil War, in which I had fought as a young soldier for the independence of Biafra.

I could not imagine how I would now, as a blind person, freely move around in the country. I could only speculate how the cities and, in particular, my little village in the bush would look today, since the war ended nine years ago. I was tremendously anxious about my travel to the country. I made rigorous and solid arrangements for people to help me coordinate my itinerary throughout my stay in the country.

On 3 March 1978, I packed up my things and departed for Nigeria on my research journey. I had extensive luggage, which contained all the essentials for my field research work.

I equipped myself with adequate supply of clothing and other personal belongings to last for the period of my stay in the country. But the greater part of my luggage was made up of different kinds of presents, which I was taking with me for my family in the village, whom I had not met for so many years.

I flew from Vienna to Lagos. Our plane arrived at the Lagos International Airport at five o'clock in the morning. Even though it was still very early in the morning, I was nevertheless greeted by an unimaginable tropical heat wave, which I was no longer used to. At the moment, I thought I was loosing my breath. But I quickly recovered from my shock when we entered into the air-conditioned arrival hall. A representative of the Nigerian National Red Cross was already there at hand to help me. The Austrian National Red Cross had informed the representatives of their counterpart in Nigeria about me and my journey before my arrival in the country.

As I had to continue my journey to the eastern part of the country, the representative of the Nigerian National Red Cross assisted me to the local airport in Lagos. I flew from there to the local airport in Port Harcourt in Eastern Nigeria. On arrival, a staff member of the Airport Authorities in Port Harcourt kindly helped me to hire a taxi to take me straight to my village in Umuahia.

We drove sixty kilometres northerly from Port Harcourt until we reached my village in Umuahia. It was a journey of about one and a half hours. When we arrived in Umuahia, I took over the responsibility of instructing the driver how to get to my village.

Before I knew it, I was applying fully the power of the mind's eye in the circumstance. From what I could tell, the landscape had not changed in any way. From my vantage point, the roads from the Umuahia town to my village were still the same.

The driver was surprised at the precision of my description of the roads and the accuracy of the directions I was giving him. After driving through a number of neighbouring villages, which I unerringly named, we finally arrived in my village, Akpahia Azumiri Umuezechiala.

But when we hit the edge of my village, I ordered the driver to drive slowly so that I could calculate the exact position of our family house as I remembered it in my mind's eye. When we finally got to the right level along the road, I immediately ordered the driver to stop the car because we had arrived at my destination, which was in the front of our family house.

It was in the early afternoon, and the whole village was very quiet and seemed to be empty. But I heard a few children playing in front of the houses on both sides of the road. When the car stopped and they saw us, they abruptly stopped playing, as if they wondered whom we might be. Certainly, the driver and I were total strangers to them.

The driver stepped out of the car and enquired of the children if we were at the right place. Before he could get the desired information from the children, an elderly lady walked cautiously towards us. She politely asked me to remove my sunglasses so that she could have a clearer view of my face, and then she immediately recognized me. She screamed out of joy. When other people in the neighbourhood heard her, they hurriedly came to greet me.

Everyone was screaming and shouting. Some were even crying. I asked about my stepmother Ngaloze and other family relatives. They said they had gone to the farm fields, as it was at the height of the farming period. Others had gone to the markets. But the people sent out message to all of them wherever they were, informing them that I had come home.

I did not ask about my mother Elizabeth Egobeke, because I knew she had been living in another village, since the break-up of her marriage with my father a long time ago. So I asked one of my relatives to send a message to her about my visit.

Meanwhile, I had to settle the fare with the taxi driver, and I also had to sign a paper for him to attest to the airport authorities in Port Harcourt that he had driven me home to my village in Umuahia.

As the news of my homecoming spread, people began streaming to my family house to greet me. At first, they could not believe that it was I. It was like a miracle to them that I had come back to them alive. Every one of them first stood at a little distance from me, watching me, before coming closer to embrace me. This happened almost without exception. I felt they thought they were seeing my ghost. But after embracing me and exchanging words with me, then they truly believed it was I. They were all genuinely full of great joy, which quickly escalated into spontaneous singing and dancing by the women, men, and children of the village.

Meanwhile, my stepmother, her sons Ogbonna and Okezie, and other family members had returned from the farm and from the market. I knew that my father had died shortly after the end of the war in 1970. I was so sad that he was not among the people who had come to welcome me home. My father should have lived to see this ... to see me standing in the middle of our compound alive and well. I demanded to see where he was buried. According to the people's custom, it was the role of the eldest man in the village to perform that task. The old man took me to the spot where my father was buried. I observed that my father's house had fallen and levelled to the ground. It had been built with sticks and mud, and its roof had been thatched with mats knitted from palm leaves. It was the family house in which I had grown up. It was beneath this debris that my beloved father now lay.

I asked the old man to tell me how my father was positioned in the grave. He showed me the direction in which his head lay. Then, I squatted down, and began to talk to my father in my mind. I told him that I was all right, and that I had come to visit home, but ... As I spoke, my eyes were filled with tears, and I began to cry silently. The old man quickly urged me to stop crying, because the other people watching us had begun to cry too.

The old man said that, if crying were the solution, my father would be with us now, because they had cried a lot when he died. The old man said that death was an important phase in our lives. It was a natural process, which we would all have to go through in our lives. We were born to live and subsequently die, so that the natural process would be glorified and perfected.

By this time, I had stopped crying. I listened intently to the old man. He then added slowly that he was looking forward to embracing death when it was his own time to die. We seemed to be sad when we were about to die. In reality, none of us was afraid of our certain death, as it was an inescapable event of the natural process. Indeed, we were only anxious about all of our beloved ones whom we would be leaving behind when we died, the old man continued sagaciously. He further told me that my father was heartbroken when he watched other sons of the village returning home from the war, and I was not one of them.

Until his death, my father had constantly asked my comrades if they had seen me and when they thought I would return home. The old man then took me by the hand and assisted me out of my father's grave. As we walked gingerly towards the people who had been watching us, I reflected deeply on these kind words of wisdom from the eldest man of my village.

Although it was already dark in the evening, I noticed that more people had gathered in our compound to join in the celebrations, which went on well into the night. The people were singing and dancing. Even though I was terribly tired and very sleepy after the long journey from Europe, I could not resist staying up with them until the last guest had departed for the night.

In the following days and nights, more people continued coming to visit me. Some had come from the neighbouring villages. Others had come from very faraway places, having heard about me. They all wanted me to tell them the story of how I managed to survive the war.

It was a very tedious narrative exercise, as I had to tell my story again and again whenever a new group of guests arrived to greet me. I recounted how I was flown to Austria and how the medical doctors failed to restore my vision.

I told them about my attendance of a school for the blind and a secondary school for adults. I also told them how my present visit was connected with my studying at the university in Vienna. They wondered how I could travel on my own from Austria to Nigeria.

The more I recounted my story to them, the wider their mouths and eyes opened with astonishment. One elderly man said I was a spirit. Another man said I was a magician. My story sounded to them like a fairy tale. They could not imagine that a blind person could ever perform all the things that I was telling them.

After spending many days in the village, with all the celebrations of my homecoming and the recounting of my story to the people, I packed up my luggage and research equipment to embark on the next stage of my journey. I asked one of my cousins Anthony Nodirim, to accompany me on the trip.

We took a train from Umuahia, to the coastal city of Port Harcourt in the southeast of the country. My mother had made arrangements, from where she was living, for me to stay there with relatives in their house throughout the duration of my field research work in the city.

Our journey from Umuahia to Port Harcourt—a distance of sixty kilometres—lasted over three hours. It was a very slow train, which stopped at any station along the route, and delayed at the stations for long periods of time.

Whilst we were sitting on the train, a man passed by the aisle begging for money. He was appealing to the people for help. He had lost his sight in the Civil War.

I was deeply moved by the pitiable condition of the blind man. I took out a twenty-Naira bank note (about thirty U.S. dollars) from my wallet and asked Anthony to give it to him. But he told me I had given him too much, thinking that I did not know the value of the note.

He said that the people were merely giving the blind man a few Kobos (that is, a few U.S. cents). But I told him that I knew exactly how much I had given him. I firmly insisted that he should give the money to the blind man. So when the blind man came round again with his appeal for help, I strongly ordered Anthony to give the man the money. Anthony stood up and reluctantly gave the money to him.

I was sitting by the window, enjoying the cool, fresh air, which was blown into the train. But my attention was interrupted by the voice of the blind man in the aisle. I suspected that apparently he did not know how much money I had given to him. So I asked Anthony to tell him how much money he had given to him. As soon as the train stopped at the next station, the blind man hurriedly got off the train and disappeared from sight. But one thing he did not know until today was that the person who gave him the twenty-Naira bank note was a blind man like him.

I was well received by my relatives when I finally arrived in Port Harcourt. They generously hosted me in their house. Most important, they helped me a great deal with the logistics for my research work in the city. It was very crucial support, as they helped me easily travel around the city to meet different kinds of people and conduct interviews with them for my research.

After spending a couple of days with my family in Port Harcourt, I thanked them for their generous hospitality and support, and departed with my accompanying relative for the cities of Warri and Sapele in the Delta region in the south of the country. I had arranged to stay with Joe Zulu, a friend of mine, in their family house in Sapele, from where I could travel easily to the neighbouring cities and towns for my field research work.

We first travelled northwards by bus, crossing the bridge over River Niger at the cities of Onitsha and Asaba, and then southwards to Warri and Sapele at the Niger delta on the Atlantic coast. I had chosen the region as the main base for my field research because of the competency of its inhabitants in speaking English-based Nigerian pidgin and creole.

When we arrived in Sapele, my friend received me cordially. Without wasting any time, I set myself to work. I went to the palm wine houses, private homes, and the busy streets to interview the people. I encouraged them to tell me stories—folklore, fairy tales, and personal experiences.

The interviews were in the form of discussions and narrations. The people felt at ease with me because I was one of their compatriots. Although some of the people felt at first shy talking to me in front of the microphone, they finally felt relaxed and opened up to me.

For example, one informant in a palm wine house wanted to know if I was an American CIA agent before he collaborated with me. I told him that I was a fellow Nigerian, not an American CIA agent. I immediately remembered one of the many reasons that my university professor considered me suitable for the field research work in Nigeria. As a Nigerian, it was much easier for me to obtain the essential data from the inhabitants for the research work.

After several weeks of hard work with very cooperative informants, I left the region to visit other major towns and cities of the country in order to have a complete overview of the linguistic feature of the Nigerian pidgin.

To conclude my research trip, I stopped over in the city of Ibadan, where I visited the Department for the Indigenous Languages at the University to apprise myself of the status of linguistic studies in Nigeria. One of my cousins, Osita Uwalaka, and his family generously hosted me in their house during my stay at the university campus. But, whilst I was conferring with the dean of the university, rioting students forcefully broke into his office. They smashed furniture and tore down his photograph from the wall. There was total confusion and anarchy on the campus; in fact, there was news of student protests in all the Nigerian universities. I was forced to curtail my stay at the university campus. I telephoned the Nigerian Red Cross in Lagos to arrange for my quick return flight to Austria.

I left Ibadan with Anthony by car to Lagos. When we arrived in Lagos, a representative of the Nigerian Red Cross was already available to receive me. He arranged for me to be driven to the Lagos International Airport by the society's official car. However, we were unable to drive through the regular road to the airport because of the student riots. We finally braved the dangers and drove to the airport, so that I did not miss my flight. As we drove along the road to the airport, we passed smashed and burning vehicles on both sides of the road. There were dead bodies lying everywhere. I held my breath throughout our journey to the airport.

I was not so much worried about my life. I was mainly concerned about the research material I had worked so hard to collect. I wanted to make sure that it all arrived safely at my university in Vienna. I only calmed down, and my worries only settled, when I finally found myself sitting on the plane in the air en route to Europe with my final destination Vienna, Austria.

I heaved a deep sigh of great relief when our plane touched down at the Vienna International Airport. Renate and Esther, who was only two and a half years old, had come to meet me at the airport. I kissed and hugged them. I was very happy to be home and to be reunited with my family at last.

I was especially glad that my precious treasures, the research material I had collected in Nigeria, had been rescued. I had arrived safely with them to Austria. As we drove home to our family flat in the 3rd district of the city of Vienna, I recounted the recent dramatic phase of my ordeal in Nigeria to Renate. She was equally happy that I had returned home safely to Austria.

In the following months, I worked laboriously on my raw research material from Nigeria. It was made up of recordings on audiotapes of over eighty informants. These informants belonged to different social and tribal backgrounds, and belonged to different age and professional groupings.

I listened and analyzed each recording, extracting and transcribing the relevant texts into Braille. The nature of the interviews was conversational and narrative, with the topics of conversation ranging from folklore and fairy tales to current affairs.

For each of the over eighty informants, I had made a fifteen-minute recording. The audiotapes also included recordings of pidgin broadcasts from the radio and television, as well as a collection of pidgin extracts from magazines, books, and newspapers.

After transcribing the texts into hundreds of Braille pages, I typed them out in normal print with my portable typewriter. But I was faced with the usual problem of how to correct my typographical mistakes in the process, as I was now living in our private apartment, and no longer had the aid of the students at the hostel.

I was permitted to write my thesis in English, even though scientific works at the Vienna University were generally written in German. My professor and other experts in our linguistic department approved the approach, given the unique linguistic nature of the subject.

Luckily, I met a Roman Catholic priest who lived in our neighbourhood. When I told him about the challenges I was facing in writing my doctoral thesis in English, he was very sympathetic with me, and immediately organized for me a pool of volunteer readers made up of upper grade students of the English class in the grammar school where he taught.

For several months, at the end of their daily school activities, these young students took turns coming to our home to help me. They read the texts to me, and helped me to correct the typographical errors in the texts. I was greatly thankful to these young students for their generous and enthusiastic support, which greatly facilitated my task of writing and editing the text of my doctoral thesis in a flawless print.

I submitted my doctoral thesis in a timely manner to my professor for corrections and approval. I felt on top of the world when he summoned me to his office to defend my research findings and scientific postulations, after he had read and made corrections to the text.

I had found out that the Nigerian pidgin was a product of socio and linguistic configuration in a heterogeneous society, which had many cultural and language groupings. My findings matched those of other scholars, which attested that such an environment was generally conducive to the development of a *lingua franca*—common language—that would enable the members of the community to communicate and interact with one another.

The Nigerian pidgin was as complex as the community that utilized it, which was relatively large. I found out that there were many varieties of the language, ranging from pidgin proper to impure and hyper anglicized pidgin.

I provided an extensive account of the various aspects of the Nigerian pidgin, covering its development, the distribution of the speech community, its characteristic features, and its relation to other English-based pidgins and creoles in West Africa. I defended effectively the reasons I had exclusively restricted my study of the Nigerian pidgin to complex sentence structures. I considered the approach to be most appropriate in revealing the separate development of the Nigerian pidgin and the magnitude of its affinity with the model language. I also wanted to prove the argument that the linguistic phenomenon of complex syntactic structures was inherent in contact vernaculars, as well as in natural languages.

I utilized fully the instruments of the modern linguistic

methodology of generative transformational grammar in the study. I discovered that the Nigerian pidgin grammar, in contrast to standard English, lacks subtlety in generating complex sentences.

However, I argued that it was not an insurmountable handicap, as the pidgin grammar quite easily compensates for that by way of circumlocution. It also borrows syntactic structures and lexical items from sources other than the model language. I argued that pidgin sentences could be simply defined as simplified complex.

Nigerian pidgin is partly influenced by the indigenous Nigerian languages in its complex sentence structure, but, in effect, it has undergone its own separate development. In complex sentence structure, it is neither in complete affinity with the indigenous languages or with standard English.

I substantiated that finding with the linguistic phenomenon of verb serialization as one of the many instances of substratum influence on the sentence structure of the Nigerian pidgin. I gave an in-depth account of the smallest and the largest units of the clause sequence, especially the functions of the continuatives, in the sentence.

I described other aspects of the clause sequence, such as the implications of negation and the system of clause coordination. But I was selective in my treatment of the subject of clause subordination, because my main concern was to point to particular aspects of the pidgin complex sentence structure.

The Nigerian pidgin grammar utilizes 'wey', 'sey', and 'make' as special markers for clause subordination, which are original English words, but have been assimilated into the Nigerian pidgin in the course of the pidginisation process. As in standard English, subordinate conjunctions are used in clauses of condition, concession, relation, purpose, and also in direct and indirect discourse.

I selectively provided a juxtaposition of Nigerian pidgin and its model language, in which I carefully mapped the constructions of ellipses and coordination of clauses in pidgin with those of the standard language. I argued that this kind of structural comparison illuminated the separate development of the pidgin from standard English. I maintained that the overlapping of certain structures should not be viewed as weakness, but as a revelation of the origin of the Nigerian pidgin English.

I gave a synoptic overview of the historical developments in pidgin and creole studies. By way of analytic description, I endeavoured to point to the believable points and inconsistencies of the hypothesis and the controversies between the proponents of monogeneticity (basically, having a single source) and polygeneticity (having many sources) and language universality as to the origin of pidgin and creole languages. But, I did not hesitate to give my own opinion in those discussions.

At the conclusion of the colloquium session in defence of my thesis, my professor got up from his seat and walked over to me and shook my hand. He congratulated me for a task excellently accomplished.

But, although I successfully completed all the required lecture units for my doctoral degree programme in addition to writing my thesis, I could not register immediately for the *rigorosum* (oral doctoral examination) at the end of the summer semester 1979 because I had completed my studies earlier than was prescribed in the university rules and regulations. I had to take pro forma courses for one more semester.

One day, while I was travelling on a tram to attend one of those pro forma courses, a ticket controller entered the train. He walked along the aisle asking the passengers for their tickets. I did not notice him at first, because I stood by the open window to enjoy the early summer cool breeze. Suddenly, the ticket controller tapped me on the shoulder and began reproaching me, giving me no chance to respond whatsoever. 'You can't travel black' (*schwarzfahren* in German), he said in a raised voice, meaning that I could not be on the train without a valid ticket. 'Perhaps, in your country, you can travel black (*schwarzfahren* in German), not here.' He continued authoritatively, drawing the attention of the other passengers.

I was somewhat astounded but very amused by his behaviour. I quickly responded by asking him, 'Isn't it my natural right to travel black? I can only travel black. I can't travel white.' I then took out my train ticket identity card and showed it to him. He looked at it studiously and said, 'Oh, you can travel with this.' I sensed that the passengers were smiling at us.

On leaving the train at the next stop, the controller again tapped me gently on the shoulder and said, 'But comrade, you have a sense of humour.' Even when he retired from service, I often met him while walking my dog in our district where he also lived. He always stopped, talked, and joked with me.

Meanwhile, with the help of my army of young volunteer readers from the grammar school in our neighbourhood, I retyped the text of the thesis to incorporate the corrections by my professor

But before I registered for the rigorosum, I had to obtain the oral agreement of my professor and the second support officer, which they did not hesitate to give to me. Thereafter, I submitted the appropriate administrative forms, documents, and my thesis in a timely manner to the dean's office. The experts had adequate time to assess and write their opinions about my work.

I was very delighted when I finally received the official notification of acceptance of my thesis, as it was the prerequisite for my admission to the rigorosum. The rigorosum consisted of two parts. In the first and principal part, I was examined on the subject of my thesis. In the second part, I was examined on the subject that had been determined by the dean of academic affairs after consultations with me, based on its relevance to the topic of my thesis. The dean of academic affairs chaired the examination panel.

After my successful examination, I was awarded the degree of doctor of philosophy by the dean of academic affairs of the University of Vienna. The date for the doctoral ceremonial award was set for 20 December 1979, and was to take place in the ceremony hall of the main building of the University of Vienna.

As I prepared for my graduation day and the celebrations thereafter, I was amazed at the sheer number of postcards from friends and well-wishers congratulating me for my achievement. I had but little time to think about the significance of it all. I never considered that all of my hard work for these achievements was something special. On the contrary, in my subconscious, I was simply trying to catch up with the opportunities that had been unjustly stolen from me in the past. When I had my vision, I had always wanted to attend a grammar school and university. But, sadly, I could not pursue these ambitions of my youth due to circumstance beyond my control at that time.

I was full of joy on that day as my family and I drove to the doctoral award ceremony at the University of Vienna. Sitting in the car, I thanked God and man for helping me to succeed in my ambitions. It occurred to me that whatever God had preserved for anyone, he would give it to them, no matter when, where, or in what condition. He had preserved these goals of my ambition for me, and had given them to me unreservedly. Blindness and its consequences could not prevent me from attaining my heavenly preserved goals in any way.

EPISODE THREE

The Stolen Times

It was around half past seven in the early morning of Tuesday, 12 November 1968. At the moment, there was not sufficient time to grab anything to eat. It had been a bitter weekend with the ceaseless firing of guns and exploding of bombs, which continued the whole day on Monday. The night was the worst of it all.

But on Tuesday morning, the bombs and gunfire had died down temporarily. It was threateningly silent, an atmosphere which could be fittingly described as the 'jungle of ghosts'. One could smell only death and fear in the air.

We did not have the slightest time to look for something to eat. Instead, we hurriedly moved to our final briefing location to assemble our equipment to proceed to the next firing line, which was a few hundred metres away from us.

As we were checking through our routine operational procedures, one of the detonators of the *Ogbunigwe*—the mass killer bomb—exploded in our midst. I was directly facing the device when it exploded. We were extremely lucky that, at the moment, the detonator device was connected only to the battery and not to the main Ogbunigwe explosive. Otherwise, the impact of the explosion would have been tremendous, and would have inflicted much more destruction to our troops.

Nonetheless, the explosion caused many casualties among my comrades, as I learned the following day in hospital. Some of them lost their fingers, and others sustained serious wounds in their faces. Some had minor wounds in the abdomen and chest.

As for me, I lost my vision instantly, since I received the full blast of the explosion in my face and chest. A large number of tiny flying metal fragments pierced through my eyes, chest, heart, and lungs. I was deafened by the impact of the explosion. I thought I was already dead. I did not know where I was anymore. But, as I learned later, two of my comrades dragged me out of the firing line and off the battlefield to a roadside. They organized a bicycle and sat me on it. One of them walked along beside me with his hand over my shoulder and held me by the hand, lest I fall down. The other comrade pushed the bicycle until we arrived at the nearest first aid post.

I was transferred to a military ambulance vehicle, which drove me straight to the Biafran armed forces hospital in Ohafia for emergency surgery. When I woke up the following morning, after recovering from the effects of anaesthesia, I found myself lying in a hospital ward that was filled with wounded comrades. Since my eyes were bandaged, I could only hear some of them crying with pain. I heard the doctors and nurses walking around and talking to the patients. They finally reached my bedside, and the doctor removed the bandages that covered my eyes.

I tried to see what was going on around me. But I could not see anything whatsoever. I then feared that my vision might have been temporarily damaged. I hung my hopes on the ability of the doctors to restore my vision in a few days.

Meanwhile, a young boy of about fifteen years of age Chidike, from the vicinity of Ohafia, volunteered to guide me. I had met him in the war front; he was one of the many courageous boys of his age attending to the needs of the fighting soldiers. He was a very clever and an intelligent young boy. He had accompanied me after my injury from the war front to the hospital.

I waited and waited. As days and weeks passed by in the hospital, my vision did not come back to me. Each time I asked the doctors when I could have my vision back, they simply told me not to worry, I would be all right. But after several weeks, I was no longer able to suppress my frustration and disappointment, and to continue believing what the doctors told me. I could not imagine how I could be blind the rest of my life, considering my young age. I began to have sleepless nights. My head was full of negative thoughts. I came to the conclusion that my life was no longer worth living. I asked my young assistant to fetch me my rucksack, in which I had all my personal belongings, including my pistol.

But the young boy seemed to have understood my intentions, because he knew that I had my pistol in the rucksack. I guessed he had suspected correctly that I was probably going to take my own life as a soldier. For the first time in our encounter, the young boy declined to carry out my instructions.

One day, several days before Christmas, I heard the doctors and the nurses walking through the ward on their daily routine, interviewing the patients. When they came to me, I noticed among the doctors a male voice that I had not heard before. The new doctor examined my eyes and my other wounds. From his accent, I figured immediately that he was a European doctor. After the routine inspection, the doctors, including the European one, left the ward and returned to the main office.

My young assistant told me that the European doctor was from the International Red Cross. Later, before the European doctor left our hospital for other places, he came to our ward and walked over to me. He introduced himself to me as Sjouke Bakker, a field medical doctor from the International Red Cross, and asked me if I would like to go to Austria in Europe with him for medical treatment. I was taken away by that question. I immediately, without hesitation, answered that I would gladly go.

He told me that he had written down my name among the patients to be flown abroad to Europe for medical treatment. Before he departed, he promised to come back, after he had visited other hospitals to select other patients for the medical trip abroad.

I was filled with tremendous excitement over the news of my journey abroad for medical treatment. It was a nice surprise Christmas present for me. For days and days thereafter, everyone in the hospital congratulated me on the news.

One late morning in January 1969, the doctors and the nurses walked through the ward on their routine visits. But the doctors suddenly stood beside my bed, as one of them examined my eyes and my other wounds. He was the Biafran area eye doctor. The hospital in Ohafia belonged to his zone of responsibility.

After the ward inspection, the doctors returned as usual to the main office for a meeting. I was one of their topics of discussion, as I was the only patient who had been selected from the Biafran Armed Forces Hospital in Ohafia for medical treatment abroad.

The Biafran eye doctor had to give his clearance for me to be flown abroad for the medical treatment. I instructed my young assistant to position himself unostentatiously close to the doctors' meeting room. He reported back to me after the meeting that the Biafran eye doctor had vehemently argued against my being flown abroad. He said that, according to his examination, my wounds were so deep and devastating that no more rescue operation would be meaningful. But the European doctor challenged his argument, insisting that it would still be very meaningful for me to be flown to Europe for medical treatment. He argued that, even if the doctors in Europe could not restore my sight, I would still have opportunities to learn a meaningful occupation. At the end of the meeting, the Biafran eye doctor agreed and signed the clearance document.

Throughout the months of January and February, I waited anxiously for news updates. It was rumoured that we could not be flown out because of the air blockade of Biafra by the Nigerian air force. Meanwhile, the battlefield in the Afikpo sector of the war was rapidly moving closer and closer to our location in the hospital. The sound of explosions and artillery gunfire seemed closer every day.

On one morning in March, the artillery bombs began falling near the premises of the hospital. By the afternoon, the bombs were already falling in and around the hospital. The hospital administration ordered immediate evacuation of the patients and the staff to Umuahia, the new headquarters of the Biafran armed forces. It was a very hopeless operation, however. The two main asphalt roads from Ohafia to Umuahia, either through Uzuakoli or Bende, had been blocked in both directions. They had been declared war fronts, and vehicles, other than those of the military, were no longer permitted to drive through those roads.

As the explosions intensified, with parts of the hospital buildings destroyed, my young assistant and I collected my rucksack and hurriedly escaped to the village. Some of the patients and staff of the hospital were with us. I did not know what happened to those patients who had to be left behind in the hospital because their conditions rendered them unmoveable.

My young assistant Chidike was very knowledgeable of the villages in Ohafia as he had been born and bred in the neighbourhood. We took a bush path, and walked through the countryside of Bende until we arrived in Umuahia. It was a journey of about thirty-two kilometres.

A military transport vehicle picked us up from Umuahia and drove us to the Biafran Armed Forces Hospital in Nkwerre. I was extremely happy when we arrived in Nkwerre, as we were no longer in immediate danger. But I was told that Nkwerre was not the final assembling place for the patients who were flying abroad for medical treatment.

After a roll-call of the patients, we were driven in a military transport vehicle to Ekwerazu. We were lodged at the Ekwerazu Girls' Secondary School to wait for our imminent departure to Europe. But our journey was repeatedly postponed due to the continued strangling blockade of Biafran air space by the Nigerian Air force.

While we continued waiting for the news about our flight to Europe, I asked my young assistant to accompany me to my village, since it was not too far away from Ekwerazu. We arrived in my village on a Friday at the end of March.

I was very happy to meet my father and my mother, as well as other relatives and people of the village. My father was devastated when he saw that I was blind. But I tried to comfort him and to allay his fears that I would be useless in life.

I told my father that I had been selected to go to Austria in Europe for medical treatment. I was pretty sure that the doctors over there would be able to restore my vision. He seemed somewhat uncertain about my optimism. He placed his hands on my head and gave me a fatherly blessing that my dreams would come true.

I spent the night in the village with my family. On Saturday, very early in the morning, I could hear a large number of adult men marching loudly through my village to the warfront, which was no longer far away. After breakfast, I quickly left the village with my young assistant and returned to our camp in Ekwerazu.

That same night, my village was turned into a battlefield, and the people fled in different directions. I was extremely lucky that I had not spent Saturday night in my village. Otherwise, I would have had to flee to some inaccessible place, from where it would not have been possible for me to link up with my group in the camp in Ekwerazu for our departure to Europe. I could have missed my heavenly blessing, which I would have lived to bitterly regret. But, thank goodness, this did not happen. Instead, on 1 May 1969, we were driven from our camp in Ekwerazu to the Biafran Uli-Ihiala airport, from where we were flown out of Biafra to Europe that night by the International Red Cross.

But before our plane took off, we spent some time at the Uli-Ihiala airport for the final administrative controls by the Red Cross and the Biafran military authorities. As we waited for the completion of these procedures, I focused my mind on my present condition, which I hoped was temporary and would be corrected by the doctors as soon as I arrived in Austria.

I considered my present condition as the climax of the unfortunate chain of events that had continued to deprive me of the opportunities to fulfil my ambitions. These opportunities had been openly stolen from me many times and in many places.

In January 1961, after the primary school, I could not

enter a secondary school to continue my education like other boys and girls of my age from the rich families. As an ordinary village farmer, my father produced only the foods that we consumed in the family. My father's earnings from selling agricultural goods sufficed only to enable us to buy from the market the things we could not produce ourselves on our farm. These extra earnings were so little that my father could not send me to a secondary school.

He was very sad and highly disappointed that he did not have the monetary means to send me to college like other clever and ambitious boys in the village. The high financial cost of a secondary school was prohibitive for my father to absorb. In his desperation, he approached many of his immediate and distant relations for help, but without success. But one of his relations, a cousin of mine Shedrack Umunna, asked me to join him in the township of Aba, where he worked as a sales clerk for a British colonial trading company.

He told my father that, while I lived with him, he would send me to a commercial school, where I would learn touch typewriting and bookkeeping. My father agreed with my cousin's offer, because he did not want to see me stay behind in the village.

Although my father greatly valued the labour support I was able to provide on the farm, he seemed relieved that at least I could now continue my education somehow. His preference, however, would have been for me to enter a secondary school right away.

In early January 1961, I went to live with my cousin in Aba. I was only sixteen years old. At twenty-two years of age, my cousin was not much older than me, but he was already an adult earning a living, and I was still considered a youngster. My cousin was just like a big brother to me. I was especially grateful to him for his generosity in caring for me while I served him in return at our relatively young ages.

When I arrived at the Aba railway station from Umuahia, my cousin came to meet me. We walked from the railway station down to the main road where he stopped a taxi to drive us into the township. It was not difficult for us to get a taxi right away because I was not carrying much luggage, except a travelling bag in which I had stuffed my clothing and some of my favourite novels.

As we drove through the township, I observed that its layout was not much different from that which I had seen in Umuahia. The taxi finally stopped at 197 Jubilee Road, where my cousin lived. My cousin paid the driver the money he demanded for our fare, and we crossed a wooden board, which had been placed over the gutter, and walked to the veranda and then into the corridor of the building. The veranda was also referred to as the front yard.

There were doors on both sides of the corridor, which led into single and double rooms of the tenants. My cousin's room was located close to the end of the corridor. He unlocked the door, and we entered. It was a large room with a medium-sized window overlooking the main yard. Below the window was a large window seat with a cushion on it. Directly in front of me, along the wall, was a big, fancy cupboard that held a big Pye radio receiver and some piles of books.

There was a long curtain to my left, which spanned from one end of the wall to the other and rose halfway up to the ceiling. It divided the room into two unequal parts. Behind the curtain was a Vono bed, which was wide enough for the sleeping comfort of two adults.

At the foot of the bed was a pantry, a small cupboard, in which food could be kept. Between the pantry and the bed hung a plastic wardrobe. In the centre of the room stood the dining table.

The floor was covered with a linoleum carpet that could be polished with beautiful designs on it. There were curtains hanging on the sole window and the entrance door. I quickly identified available spaces in the room, and very carefully arranged my meagre belongings in one corner. Then I walked out to explore the rest of the building, as it was going to be my new dwelling place.

From the end of the corridor, I entered into the main yard. It was a huge space, surrounded with very high walls. The building was divided into different sections. Our room was in one of the sections that faced the road, in which the tenants lived in the single or double rooms.

The male tenants traded in second-hand clothes, and the women in foodstuff. Other youngsters like me, who were living with them, were learning the trades. The landlord and his family occupied the other section in front of me on the left as I stood in the main yard. It was a big apartment with its own veranda. The other section was on my right-hand side. It was the common kitchen. Each tenant and the wives of the landlord had a space allocated to them in the kitchen for cooking and storing firewood.

Further away from the side of the kitchen area were two smaller rooms which were the sanitary facilities for all the occupants of the building. One of them was the bathing room, and the other housed the bucket latrine. At the end of the main yard, there was a small iron gate that opened onto the backyard, which was also referred to as the half-line.

The town planners of the British colonial administration had been exceptionally creative in designing the layout of the township. Pedestrians did not have to utilize the road junctions to cross from one street to the other. The spaces and the half-lines between the buildings provided shortcuts for easy movement around the township. They also facilitated the laborious work of those who collected the night soil from the bucket latrines.

After I settled down and could move around the township

easily, my cousin registered me at the Inyamah's Commercial Institute, which was housed in a normal township building at 21 Pound Road. The institute occupied the rooms in the front section of the building.

We were male and female students. We sat in the various rooms according to our grades and subjects of study. The atmosphere at the institute was almost similar to that in a traditional college.

We were taught secretarial skills in shorthand and touch typewriting, as well as bookkeeping according to the syllabus standards of Pitman's of London. I was terribly fascinated to learn how to type without looking at my fingers or the keyboard, with all my fingers in the correct places. Within a few months of practice, I made fewer mistakes and greatly increased my typing speed. I also enjoyed our lessons in bookkeeping, in which I learned how to keep and balance the account sheets. My ambition was to be able to take the Pitman's examination to acquire the Royal Society of Arts (RSA) diploma in all the subjects of our study.

At the institute, the lessons usually began at nine o'clock in the morning, and ended two o'clock in the afternoon from Monday to Friday. Before I went to my lessons, I woke up very early in the morning and fetched two buckets of bathing water from the public taps for my cousin and me. I then made a fire in the kitchen and prepared our breakfast. When I returned from the lessons, if needed, I went to the market to buy food with the money my cousin had given to me. Then I prepared our meal.

At the weekends, I swept our big room clean, dusted, cleaned, polished the furniture, and polished the floor before I went outdoors to play football with the other boys, or to swim at the Waterside. These were my part of responsibilities in our common household in return for the support that my cousin was giving to me.

My training at the Inyamah's Commercial Institute did not last for long. It suddenly came to an abrupt end in October 1961 when my cousin was transferred to another branch of his company in Onitsha. I went with him, and when we arrived, we were the only tenants in the house in which we were to live. It was a family house, near to the main market on the River Niger. The landlady cordially welcomed us as if we were members of her own family. We lived in a comfortable room, and shared the parlour and other common areas of the house with members of the landlady's family.

But, even though I enjoyed the comfort of our new dwelling place, I was extremely anxious, since my cousin did not make any effort to register me at a commercial institute in Onitsha so that I might continue my training. I could not understand what might have caused his change of mind, since I had been loyal to him, serving him to the best of my abilities.

Two months later, in December, we returned home to our village from Onitsha for the Christmas celebrations. My father was deeply disappointed to learn about my cousin's negligence in the matter of my training. After speaking to my cousin, my father told me that I was not returning to Onitsha after the Christmas and the New Year celebrations.

As we celebrated Christmas and the New Year, Lillian the wife of Isaac Uwalaka, the richest and most highly educated and most respected man in our village, approached my father to seek his permission for me to join her family in Aba and work in her provision store as a storekeeper.

The woman had known about my training at the Inyamah's Commercial Institute. She had also heard that I had been successful in acquiring skills in bookkeeping and accountancy, despite the relatively short period I stayed at the institute.

My father agreed with her proposal, even though my

going to work as a clerk did not impress him, and no wages were negotiated with her for my services. He simply thought that, if I lived in her family, her husband might notice me and might even offer to support my college education. But my father never approached the rich man directly about support for my college education. He thought the man had too many heavy loads on his shoulders already. He was already training four of his own children and some of his cousins at college, all at the same time.

At the beginning of the new year, I helped my father on the farm. After all the seeds were planted and the farming period was over, I went to Aba to work as a clerk. The family lived at 139 St. Michael's Road.

I met many young people when I arrived in the house. They were male and female servants of the man and his wife. There were also housemaids among them. Some of these servants were youngsters of my age, and others were a little older than me.

The retail provision store belonged to Lilian. It was located in one of the rooms of the building facing the street. The items sold in the store included household items, beverages, bakery products, and other foodstuff.

Before I began my work in earnest, I took an inventory of the articles presently available in the store, and balanced the accounts book. As I received delivery of various goods, I arranged them on the shelves, sold them to customers, and rigorously kept the daily accounts.

My duties were clearly defined. I was not involved in the work of the male and female servants in the house, unless in emergency situations. But I was surprised to observe that the children of the man and his wife were not involved in the affairs of the house. The children were not encouraged to help in the household activities. These were left to the male and female servants to perform. They went to the market, managed the finances, and purchased the food. They prepared the various kinds of meals and kept the house meticulously clean.

I always wondered how some rich parents could unwisely exclude their children from learning practical household activities, which were undeniably essential for their survival later in life. These male and female servants were draconically trained to cope with the processes of real life at the expense of the children of their employers. These youngsters might be servants today, but tomorrow they might be lords by the virtue of the knowledge they had acquired in the houses of their masters and mistresses. I could not understand why some rich parents could not strike a balance between giving their children the freedom to enjoy their wealth, and imparting parental wisdom and common sense to them for their future lives. Most children of rich parents would be obliged to acquire these skills the hard way by their own individual efforts outside their parental houses.

While I was making these observations, I waited for Isaac to recognize my presence in the house. He had seen me in the provision store selling goods as the clerk, and had also spoken to me several times in the house. But he never approached me in the manner in which my father had hoped.

After several months of no change in the man's attitude towards me, I wrote a letter to my father explaining the situation to him. My father responded promptly and instructed me to leave the job and return home immediately to our village in Umuahia. I packed up my very limited belongings and followed my father's instructions.

On one evening, a few days following my return to the village, one of our neighbours visited our home with a man Iroha, whom he introduced to my father as his brother-in-law. The man was living in Lagos and working as a big trader.

He had come home on emergency family business and would return back to Lagos shortly.

The man offered to take me along with him to Lagos, where I would live and work for him in his stores. In return, he would train me in a college. My father agreed with the offer, and I was excited about the possibility of going to a college in Lagos after all.

Two days later, I stuffed my clothes and novels into my travelling bag and went to the man's village, which was about a forty-five minutes walk from our own. Very early in the morning of the following day, we drove off in the man's car on our way to Lagos.

On the same day, in late afternoon, we arrived at the man's house in Surulere, one of the districts of Lagos. It was a one-storey mansion. Chimezie and his wife occupied the upper floor of the building. Some of their relations lived with them as their male and female servants. They kept the whole house meticulously clean at all times.

The storerooms, guest rooms, and garage for the car were all located on the ground floor. I was only marginally involved in the maintenance of the household, since I had come for another kind of business.

I had barely spent one week in the house when the man moved me to one of his trading stores at 225 Herbert Macaulay Road, formerly called King George V Avenue, Yaba. I had come to join his longest-serving storekeeper at this branch of his chain of trading stores.

The man had three such trading stores in Lagos, one each in the districts of Yaba, Idioro, and Ebute Metta. He was a very successful retail merchant, even though he could not read and write. But at least he had successfully learned to sign his name on documents.

It was said that the man had begun his career in Lagos a few years earlier by selling newspapers on the streets. He then went on as a petty trader to develop into a powerful merchant. Today, his trading stores sold a variety of goods—clothing, cosmetics, music records, and food items.

My co-worker and I received the goods as they were delivered to the shop, and sold them. I fully applied my skills in bookkeeping and accountancy in maintaining the records of the sales and other transactions, which was actually the main reason the man had brought me to his store. I always accompanied the man to the other branches of his stores to help him when he periodically inventoried his stock of goods and income.

Life for me in the store was not as pleasant and comfortable as in the man's house when I first arrived in Lagos. My co-worker and I did not have the luxury of a separate room for ourselves apart from the shop. Our pantry stood in the corridor. We cooked our food in the common kitchen and preserved it there. We shared the bathroom and the bucket latrine with the other tenants in the building. We worked in the shop during the day and slept there during the night. At the end of the business day, we simply spread out our mats on the bare floor and slept there.

Our regular opening hours were between nine o'clock in the morning and nine o'clock in the evening from Monday through Friday. As we lived and worked in the shop, we were actually available to sell goods to customers at any odd time of the day, even on the weekends. The only noticeable difference between making sales when the shop was 'closed' and making sales when it was 'open' was that, when the shop was 'closed', the loudspeakers were not blaring music ceaselessly in front of the shop.

I did not mind the hardships and the slavery conditions whatsoever because I knew that, as compensation, the man would send me to a college. I took a number of examinations for entrance into various colleges, and passed them all.

But each time I briefed the man about my success, he seemed somewhat subdued, and did not show any interest. He found an excuse to disqualify the college, either on the grounds of high financial costs or physical distance.

At the end, I concluded that the man was obviously only interested in my serving in his shop, and not in my going to a college. He did not want to lose me in his shop because his business was benefiting immensely from my skills in bookkeeping and accountancy.

As usual, I wrote a letter to my father, and explained the situation to him. My father's reply was swift. He asked me to return home immediately. I had spent almost six months with the man in Lagos.

Our hope for me to be able to attend a college had again been smashed aside. A few days before Christmas in 1962, without even demanding payment of any accumulated wages from the man, I packed up my belongings and returned to my father's house in the village in Umuahia.

In the meantime, my cousin, Daniel Iroakazi, had been monitoring my ordeal from Kaduna since I left his mother to return to my father's house in Akpahia, after completing my primary school education. He had heard about my recent experiences in Lagos and Aba.

He wrote a letter to my father and expressed his support for his efforts in my affairs, as he was especially saddened by the lack of opportunities for me to continue my education at a college level. He therefore asked me to join him in Kaduna as soon as it was practicable. Regrettably, he did not have the means to send me to a college, he explained to my father apologetically, but he would make every effort to help me to learn a good occupation while I lived with him.

My cousin's offer of support came at an auspicious moment. My father was pleasingly moved, and I was full of joy, as it was exceedingly good news for us at Christmas and for the New Year.

In early 1963, I again helped my father on the farm. And again, after all the seeds were planted and the farming season was over, I packed up my clothes and my favourite books in a modest suitcase and departed from home—this time, by train from Umuahia to Kaduna. It was a very long, overnight journey.

We travelled northwards through Enugu, crossing the River Benue at Makurdi, then westward through Kafanchan to Kaduna. We passed through beautiful landscapes of sub-tropical and savannah vegetation. I had not been on such a long journey before, despite the fact that I was now eighteen years of age. We arrived at the Kaduna railway station in the late afternoon. My cousin came to meet me at the station. At first, he could not locate me because there were too many passengers moving in all directions. I saw him, however, and walked quickly towards him. We embraced and greeted each other.

He took my suitcase from me, and I carried the bag in which I had brought presents for him from my father and his mother. We walked to a car park, where he hired a taxi to drive us to his home in the town. As we drove through the town, I observed differences in the appearance of the buildings from those in the south of the country. Kaduna was the capital of the Northern Region of Nigeria. It was the administrative headquarters of the regional government. The buildings were a mixture of southern and northern architecture. The structure of the buildings was in harmony with the Islamic religious tradition.

Finally, we arrived at 19 Argungu Road, where my cousin lived. After my cousin paid off the taxi, we went through the gate and straight to my cousin's room. It was a very large room with every piece of furniture systematically in place.

There were two Vono beds, one for me and the other one for my cousin. There were two big cupboards for glassware and similar items, a large cushion, a bookshelf, a big study table, a dining table, two single chairs, a pantry, and a hanging plastic wardrobe for our clothes. The linoleum carpet floor was meticulously clean and shiny. The room had only one door and two windows that opened onto the yard. Curtains hung down over the windows, as was customary all over the country.

The building as a whole had five sections, two of which housed the common kitchen, the bathing room, and the bucket latrine facility. The living rooms for the tenants were in the other three sections. In the yard, which was very spacious, stood three big mango trees, which kept the building and the yard cool at all times.

The tenants were ordinary citizens with various occupations. Among the tenants were three traders, a librarian, a tailor, two carpenters, two civil servants who worked in a government office, a welder, a bricklayer, and three fitters who worked in various building construction companies. Some of the tenants were married couples with children, and others were still single. They were all southerners and from the Igbo tribe, which was my own tribe. This was not an unusual social phenomenon because the citizens of Nigeria tended to live among people from their own tribes or regions. As I later found out, in Kaduna, as well as in other northern towns, there was always an area called Sabon Gari, which was an exclusive living district for immigrants, especially from the southern part of the country.

My cousin and I lived enviably in good harmony. He was like my older brother; I served him well, and he took care of my affairs as his junior brother.

After I had settled down comfortably and was able to move around the town independently, my cousin registered me as an apprentice in an electrician workshop. Before taking that action, he had discussed the matter thoroughly with me. Indeed, he had observed that I had shown special interest in electrical installations when I was living in the village with his mother.

As I attended my training in the workshop, I worked also as a junior support electrician for a professional electrician with the Electrical Contractors of Nigeria Limited, an expatriate European company in the buildings construction field. I benefited a great deal in my training by working for the company on its major electrical installations activities at the Hamdala Hotel, the Nigerian Air Force garrison, and the New Nigerian Newspaper building.

The practical experience I acquired at those construction sites accelerated and widened my knowledge of the profession immensely. I learned surface and conduit electrical wiring, and panel and mechanical electrical installation, among other things. This experienced added to what I was taught at the electrician workshop.

I became so interested in the profession that I did not want to finish my training as an ordinary electrician. I began to read books on electricity and magnetism. I visited regularly the American library and the British council library to borrow relevant books on the subject.

I was fascinated by the biographies of many thinkers and inventors, especially Benjamin Franklin. I was impressed by his invention of the lightning rod and his open field experiments with his son. I was even motivated to attempt some of these experiments on my own.

In the evenings, after work, I went to the library to read. At weekends, I rode on my bicycle with my tool kit to very quiet areas of the town. These were the areas around the Independence Way and the Race Course, where the Europeans and upper class citizens lived. I experimented on various features of electricity and magnetism, based on the things I had read in the books. Basically, before I knew it, I was teaching myself physics, and experimenting in my own mobile laboratory.

My plan was to take the City and Guilds of London professional examinations in electrical engineering externally. My targeted ambition was eventually to become an electrical engineer. As I was pursuing my ambition, the unfortunate thing happened. My plan was suddenly interrupted; indeed, I felt that it was possible I might never be able to carry it out.

In the night of Friday, 15 January 1966, we heard sounds of explosives on the northerly outskirts of the town. At the moment, we were not worried because such sounds were not unusual. Kaduna was not only the capital of the Northern Region, it was also the headquarters of the Nigerian Armed Forces. The inhabitants of the town were used to sounds of shooting and explosions made by soldiers in their training exercises.

But, on Saturday morning, as we rode on our bicycles to work at the Nigerian Air Force Base, we saw soldiers lying in the bushes in fighting positions along the road on both sides. They were dressed in camouflage uniforms and carried all their fighting gear. The soldiers pointed their guns towards us, and looked terribly threatening. They did not open their mouths to speak to us. Instead, they signalled with their hands that we should turn round and go back. From where we were, we could see the premiere's house. I looked up in front of me and saw smoke coming out of one section of the building. At the gate, there was no policeman on duty as was customary. I immediately feared that something serious must have happened.

We turned our bicycles and quickly went home. By this time, my cousin and I had moved from 19 Argungu Road to

15 Zaria Road. We then heard the announcement on the radio that the military had taken over as the governing power in the country. The event was unprecedented, since we had never heard about a military coup in Nigeria. The citizens did not know how to immediately react to the news.

In the following days and weeks, there were a lot of rumours as to who had fallen victim to the military coup. But it was officially announced in the news that the leader of the coup was a young Igbo military officer.

The northern population was not happy that none of the politicians killed in the military coup were from the Eastern Region. The civilian population waited expecting the military authorities to sort out their differences so that peace and normality would prevail throughout the country. But, by April, it seemed that the civilian population had lost patience with the military's competence in controlling the situation. Riots were reported in some northern towns, including Kaduna. The northerners had taken their vengeance for the victims of the coup against southerners, especially those from the Igbo tribe.

In the next four months, southerners, especially the Igbos, began fleeing from northern cities and towns to the Eastern Region, to escape the merciless attacks of their northern compatriots.

Meanwhile, I had been seriously considering my exodus from Kaduna, as it was no longer safe for a southerner, like me, to move around in the town. The decisive moment for me came with the second military coup on 29 July, when the northern soldiers broke out of the military barracks to join the wild civilian mob in savaging southerners in the town. Members of the ferocious civilian mob were carrying clubs, machetes, spears, and bows and arrows. But, in addition, there were soldiers among them, armed with automatic machine guns and explosives. They went from street to street, and from house to house searching for their victims and slaughtering them openly. They shouted angrily that the Igbos must go back to their region, and leave them alone. The scenes were utterly disgusting. I wondered what on earth could provoke people to lose their faculty of reasoning and inflict such cruelty and barbarism to their fellow human beings.

But I saluted the help given to us by our fellow young northern friends in that despicable situation. Indeed, they were able to convince me that genuine friendship was stronger than hatred. As young boys and as friends in Kaduna, we went together to the cinemas, played football, went to social events, and joked and laughed. These friends had given me advanced information about the plan of the angry mob to raid our street. I was hiding in our house with Victor Nwaigbo, another young friend who was also from my village in Akpahia.

Before the angry mob advanced forward to our street, our young northern friends had given us their traditional northern clothing to wear. Two of them carried our luggage and went ahead before us to the railway station. We went together with the other boys and joined the angry mob as they raided the houses and the streets.

As the mob streamed along the main road to the railway station, they hunted out men and women from their houses and in the streets. Among them were even little children, who had lost their parents in the meantime. When mob participants found them, they killed them instantly, and vandalized their belongings, chanting angry songs with satisfaction.

'What a heinous act to witness!' I muttered to myself. I was frightened out of my wits. My skin crept, and my body shook. I was horrified. I was afraid that they might discover that I was an Igbo. Or someone might betray me along the way. But this did not happen until we arrived at the Kaduna Railway Station with the angry mob, where we met a huge number of men, women, and children already waiting for the train to take them to the Eastern Region. They carried with them whatever of their belongings they could lay their hands on as they escaped from the angry mob.

We disengaged ourselves from the mob and collected our luggage from our young northern friends. There was a scene of pandemonium all over the railway station.

In the meantime, the wild northern soldiers left the angry crowd and came on to the platform. They searched for the soldiers from the Eastern Region who had escaped from the barracks. They could identify such soldiers by the style of their short military haircut. They picked up a number of them from the huge crowd of refugees and shot them dead on the spot as the terrified passengers looked on. Then they walked away to rejoin the angry mob.

We were all extremely frightened. It was a despicable, indescribable scene ... a nightmare from which I thought I would never ever recover. When the train finally arrived, it was already filled with passengers who had boarded along the way from other northern towns. I wondered how all the passengers at the station could find places on the train. But we were assured that the next train would be arriving soon. Nevertheless, my young friend and I managed to get on board the train. It was a horrible scene inside the train. People were sitting and standing on one another. Some passengers were trampled to death or suffocated. Some were even crouching on the entrance steps holding on to the handrails. As the train moved on, I observed some of these passengers falling off the train. They had become so weak and tired that they could not hold on any longer. I did not know what eventually happened to those passengers because the train never stopped until we arrived at the next station.

I was so glad that we had finally departed from Kaduna, leaving all the horrible scenes at the railway station behind us. Everyone on the train prayed for our safe return to the Eastern Region. Almost all the passengers were from the Igbo tribe.

When we arrived at Makurdi, our train was held up and was not permitted to cross the Benue Bridge. We wondered what could be wrong. We heard that some northern soldiers had boarded the train in search of fleeing southern soldiers. But, after a delay of several hours, the train was permitted to cross the Benue Bridge at Makurdi. We continued our journey southwards until we arrived at Enugu Railway Station.

Now we could tell exactly what the ferocious northern soldiers had done when our train was held up for several hours at the Benue Bridge in Makurdi. They had taken away several fleeing Igbo soldiers and shot them dead as they had done elsewhere. The body of a large man was removed from our train. The soldiers had cut of his head. The incident was broadcast on the news media.

The entire population of the Eastern Region was shocked and outraged at these inconceivable atrocities as recounted by their fellow citizens fleeing from the Northern Region. By this time, it was reported that over 30,000 easterners had been massacred in the Northern Region, and several million displaced.

It was already late in the evening when the train arrived at the Umuahia Railway Station. My young friend and I collected our luggage and made our way to our village, which was a walk of about six kilometres.

When we arrived in the village, the people were celebrating. They had been singing and dancing all day, because it was our Sunday market day. People began shouting and screaming with joy when they saw us in the village. Our safe return from the Northern Region gave added impetus to the celebrations in the village, which went on till the small hours of the morning.

In the following weeks, more and more people returned to my village and the neighbouring villages. They had all fled from the atrocities in the northern part of Nigeria. They were equally terrified and traumatized by their experiences at the hands of the angry mobs and the ferocious northern soldiers.

In the meantime, the military government of the Eastern Region established the Commission for the Resettlement of Displaced Persons from other parts of the country. Every displaced easterner was requested to register with the commission for resettlement in education and employment, or for welfare and hardship support. I went to Enugu to register with the commission.

But, before I departed for Enugu, a pleasing incident happened to me, which overshadowed the recent horrors and nightmares of my escape from Kaduna. A middle-aged lady appeared unexpectedly in the village. A neighbour introduced her to me as my mother. She was visiting the village on my behalf, but did not have the courage to come straight to my father's house. She stopped first at the neighbour's house to enquire about my sister and me.

As my sister was already married and no longer lived with us in my father's house, I hurried to meet my mother. When she saw me, she smiled broadly and ran to embrace me. She held me tight to her bosom as tears began streaming down her cheeks. I was momentarily speechless, but overjoyed, as I stood right in front of my mother. At twenty-one years of age, I was only getting to know my birth mother for the first time. I had never thought I would ever see her again in my life.

People in our village had told my sister and me a great deal about our mother. As she now stood before me, I observed that she looked exactly like me. After our brief acquaintance, I took her to my father's house, where she was cordially received.

I interrupted my travels between Enugu and Umuahia to go with my mother to the village where she had remarried and had four children. I was happy to meet my half-siblings: three boys and a girl.

Later, I went with her to visit my sister in the village where she lived with her husband. My sister was equally overjoyed and speechless when I introduced the middle-aged woman as our mother. She, too, never believed that she would ever see her birth mother again.

When I arrived in Enugu, I went straight to the Commission for the Resettlement of Displaced Persons. The offices of the commission were located in the Presidential Hotel. I registered with the commission for employment as an electrician. However, the officials of the commission could not process my application accordingly, since I did not have any certificates to prove my professional competence in the trade. They sent me to the Government Trade Centre in Enugu for me to be tested in the trade. I sat for the theoretical and practical examinations, and passed it with distinction. I thus obtained my certificate as a Government's Grade III Trade Test in Domestic and Industrial Installations. Shortly thereafter, a post of electrician was identified for me at the Afam gas power station near Port Harcourt. I was to be responsible for monitoring and servicing Transformer 18 of the facility.

My father accompanied me to Port Harcourt for the interview and inspection of the facility in Afam. I was successful at the interview, and was selected right away for the job. My father was very proud of me and my achievements. I was excited and hopeful of my impending employment as a professional electrician. I looked forward to receiving the letter of appointment from the Afam gas power station authorities. However, the south-eastern portion of Nigeria had seceded from the rest of the country and declared itself the Republic of Biafra on 30 May 1967. The Federal Military Government of Nigeria declared war against the new state— the Nigerian Civil War had begun. My chances of going to work at Transformer 18 were shattered beyond recovery. My employment at the facility was suspended indefinitely until after the war, as all young men of my age were obliged to join the Biafran Army to defend the young republic. I was no exception to that obligation.

My main motivation for joining the army was to contribute to the concerted effort of repelling those ferocious northern soldiers, whom I had encountered in my horrifying exodus from Kaduna. I knew that they were now integrated into the Nigerian Federal Army and were determined to continue their abhorrent massacre of the Igbos right in Biafraland.

I swore to myself that I would never compromise my contributions to the common effort to repel them from achieving their goal of annihilation of the people of Biafra. I was terrified at even the remotest possibility of meeting these northern soldiers again in Biafran towns and villages, including my own, should they succeed with their crusade.

I had seen these savage northern soldiers in action on the streets and at the railway station in Kaduna. I had no illusion in my mind as to the kind of stuff they were made, and what they were capable of doing to an Igbo man, woman, or child who stood in their way.

Besides, I saw that the Nigerian soldiers, waging aggressive war against the people of Biafra, now turned themselves into vandals. The Nigerian pilots were indiscriminately dropping bombs on Biafran cities, towns, and villages, massacring and killing innocent civilians in marketplaces, schools, churches, and hospitals. They were committing abominable genocide beyond all conceivable proportions against the people of Biafra.

Therefore, I was totally convinced that it was no exaggeration or overreaction to take up arms in self-defence under the circumstances. Moreover, young men of my age had no choice but to join the army, or be conscripted into it. Otherwise, one was considered to be acting against the interest of one's own people.

After my relatively short military training, I was posted to the Ikot Ekpene zone of the war operation. We came to relieve another group of our troops, who, until the day before, had been fighting a fierce battle with the federal troops.

When we arrived at the front, the battlefield was quiet. Troops on both sides were dug in around two hills that were separated by a valley through which ran a stream of water. Soldiers from both sides fetched drinking water from the stream, and it was a miracle that neither side shot at the other's water bearers. We were tacitly observing a non-negotiated agreement not to shoot at each other because we all badly needed the water from the stream. We took turns in our camp to fetch the drinking water.

One day, it was my turn to go down to the stream and fetch our drinking water. As I stood at the edge of the stream to fill my bucket with water, I noticed an enemy soldier about thirty metres away on the other side of the stream. He had also came down to the valley to fetch water from the stream. It was not an unusual scenario because sometimes we meet each other on the opposite sides of the stream while we fetched our water. But we never talked or stared at each other on such occasions. However, at this moment, the enemy soldier was staring at me, not taking his focus away from me, and not fetching his water. I became anxious and worried because I didn't know what he was up to. I briefly considered bringing down my submachine gun from my shoulder and cocking it.

I remembered that the first rule of engagement for a soldier in the battlefield was: 'He who shoots first survives.'

I watched him closely. His submachine gun was hanging over his shoulder; he was not in a threatening posture. Then he began walking towards me, as if he had something to say to me. When he had moved close enough to my position, he cautiously called out my civilian youth hangout name in a low voice: 'Smartisco!' He was not so sure that I was really the one he remembered now standing right in front of him on the opposite side of the stream.

I was very surprised to hear him address me thus because it was not my combatant nickname that was boldly and visibly written on the front of the military cap that I was wearing. My combatant nickname was the name of a popular Viet Kong guerrilla fighter, which I enthusiastically adopted when I joined the army.

I had popularly been called by the nickname 'Smartisco' among my young friends as we spent the evenings and nights together hanging out in down town Kaduna. Thus, I immediately recognized the enemy soldier, who was now standing in front of me on the opposite side of the stream. He was one of my young northern friends who helped us to escape from the angry mob and the vicious northern soldiers in Kaduna.

It was an odd and cumbersome situation as we waved and smiled at each other. Indeed, we felt momentarily so sorry for ourselves for having become the victims of circumstances that were beyond our control … circumstances that were destroying our youth. We did not talk loudly to each other; we didn't want to raise false alarm in our respective camps.

I reported the incident to my comrades when I returned to our camp. And I believe that he did the same when he returned to his camp, because no hostile action was initiated from their side following our encounter. On the contrary, whenever we went down to the stream to fetch water, we found several tins of canned food, such as corned beef, sardines, soft drinks, bread and biscuits, as well as packets of cigarettes and matches lying on our side of the stream. At first, we were suspicious of the foods, lest they be poisoned.

Later, we found out that they were making those donations to us in good faith, because they knew that their fellow victims of the war on the other side were short of food supplies and other amenities. This state of affairs between us and the enemy soldiers on the other side of the stream lasted ten days.

On the night of the tenth day, we heard noises of sustained activities in the enemy's camp. We were fully aware that we were still at war with each other, and that we must begin firing at each other soon. Those hectic movements gradually subsided long before dawn. However, we remained suspicious and kept our vigilance, as we could neither make head nor tail of the situation. In the early morning, we sent one of our comrades to go down to the stream and fetch water. We waited for him to come back, but he did not return to the camp at the expected time. We immediately suspected that something was wrong. Our comrade might have been captured but not yet killed. Otherwise, we would have heard the shooting of a gun. Or, he might have escaped through a longer route to return to our camp.

But, before we began taking precautionary action, our position came under heavy gunfire from the enemy side. We now understood what had been happening in the enemy camp the night before. The friendly group had been replaced by another group who did not understand the prevailing state of affairs between our two sides.

They shot bazooka bombs, mortar bombs, and artillery gunfire relentlessly on our position. They fired artillery bombs over our heads, seeking to cut us off from retreat.

We immediately returned the fire, but could not match their heavy assault. They were better equipped with heavier weapons. Notwithstanding, we held our ground briefly by maintaining our limited firing capacity to disrupt them from quickly constructing a pontoon to cross the stream. Meanwhile, we were able to withdraw from our positions to regroup in another location far behind, which was out of the range of their artillery bombs.

As we retreated, we carried our dead and wounded comrades with us. The enemy had inflicted heavy casualties on us, as we were outnumbered and overpowered by them.

As we regrouped, I was selected among the soldiers to be redeployed to another zone of the war operations. Some of the other soldiers remained behind to set up a new line of defence against the enemies.

Before our departure, I reflected on the bizarre situation of meeting my young northern friend in this sector of the battlefield. Providence did not want us to kill or harm each other, as his group was removed in a timely manner from the front line of the battle before the fierce gunfire and bombardment between our two sides took place.

I was redeployed to the Port Harcourt zone of the war operations. When my group arrived at the Biafran Military garrison at Ikwerre, we were informed of an impending brigade assault on the Port Harcourt International Airport.

The enemy had pushed our soldiers out of the airport, and had been occupying it for several days. As in other places, it was extremely important that we take the airport back quickly from the enemy.

During the next two days, we rehearsed our strategies for action, which had been worked out by the officers and the field commander of our war zone. It was a huge operation, to which the battle planners had committed a sizeable number of troops.

On the morning of our departure to the front line at the airport, the field commander addressed the entire brigade. The troops were highly motivated by his speech. After we had had our meals, we received soft drinks, alcoholic drinks, and cigarettes, and other commodities in generous quantities. Many of the soldiers began to consume the provisions with cupidity, especially the alcoholic drinks, the cigarettes, and other smoking materials. I was terribly horrified at their behaviour.

I cautioned some of my comrades that they should refrain from consuming their provisions, especially the intoxicating ones, until we came off the battlefield successfully. I considered it fundamentally unwise to lure soldiers with such stimulants as a means of motivating them before an impending assault.

Finally, we boarded the lorries according to our groupings, and started off to the Port Harcourt International Airport. I counted over forty-two lorries loaded with troops, weapons, and ammunition. As the lorries rolled on, the troops were excited and noisy, singing battle songs. I observed that some of them were already under the influence of some kind of drug. But they were all in good and high spirits.

Several kilometres before the airport, the lorries stopped. We disembarked and deployed, moving forward to our assault destination. We did not know that the enemy had been observing our movements all along, and had waited for us to come within a deadly zone in the circumference of the battlefield.

As soon as they could confirm their hideous plan, they opened fire at our positions. They bombarded us with mortar bombs, artillery bombs, bazooka bombs, and heavy machinegun fire. Bullets and bombs were flying everywhere like a heavy rainfall. The enemy then called in fighter planes, which not only fired bullets from above, but also dropped bombs on our positions.

It was like being in a hell. I could not raise my head to observe the environment. We were pinned down by the enemy's heavy fire. I was horrified when I managed to look up and saw some of our soldiers on their feet, braving the raining bullets and bombs to move forward.

Many of them were knocked down by the bombs or pierced through by bullets. We suffered heavy casualties. Just then, a mortar bomb fell very close to my position. I was instantly deafened by the blast, but my comrade's legs were blown off.

I moved towards him, tied tourniquets onto his legs above the wounds to limit the bleeding, took him on my back, and crawled to a safe distance, where the velocity of the bullets was not so threatening. Then I stood up and carried him on my back, praying that the bombs and bullets from the fighter planes would not hit us. I still could hear nothing.

I arrived safely with my wounded comrade at the military ambulance vehicle that was waiting at the side of the road. We were driven straight to the Biafran Armed Forces Hospital in Aba.

I later learned, while at the hospital, that we had not been able to recapture the Port Harcourt International Airport. The enemy maintained their position, and even advanced forward to push us out of our other positions in the vicinity.

I spent about ten days at the hospital until my hearing cleared up. As soon as I could hear well again, I was discharged from hospital. I immediately went on military sick leave to return to my village in Akpahia.

After the expiration of my military sick leave, I reported again for duty at the Biafran Armed Forces garrison in Afugiri, which was very close to my village. I returned every day to spend the night in the village after my day's duties at the garrison.

I contemplated joining the engineering battalion of the

Biafran Armed Forces, given my profession as an electrician in domestic and industrial installations. I thought I could be more useful to a section of the armed forces that was relevant to my professional field of occupation. But I was promptly attached to the Ogbunigwe—mass killer explosive—section of the engineering battalion. I was posted to the Afikpo zone of the war operations. As soon as I arrived at my new posting, I was given training on the job.

I was excited about my new posting and the job of operating the Ogbunigwe, which had been developed by the Biafran scientists. It was one of the highly effective defensive bombs in the weapons arsenal of the Biafran Army. The bomb was comprised of various segments: the main explosive in an encasement, the removable detonator, the battery and switch, and connecting cables.

The main explosive segment came in different sizes between 5 kilos and 500 kilos. The massive ones were transported to their locations of ignition by military lorries, and the lighter ones were carried by soldiers. We carried the batteries and the detonators with us in separate bags.

Both car and torch batteries were used for generating the electrical power. But whenever torch batteries were used, they were connected serially to each other to produce an electromotive force between 12 and 16 volts.

The detonator could only be inserted into the main segment of the explosive and connected by wires to the batteries and the switch at the moment the Ogbunigwe was ready to be launch. The batteries had to be fully charged for the operation of the Ogbunigwe to be successful. Indeed, it was a highly risky job for the operators, as is every other activity on the battlefield.

As I lay helpless in my sickbed with the injuries in my eyes in the Biafran Armed Forces Hospital in Ohafia, I reflected deeply on my recent activities on the battlefield as an Ogbunigwe operator. And, inasmuch as I saluted the ingenuity of the Biafran scientists in developing the Ogbunigwe, I bemoaned the circumstances that had necessitated the invention of this monstrous explosive in the first place. The war could have been avoided if the Nigerian federal military government had implemented the Aburi peace accord in good faith. The war, as the sole culprit of my blindness, had prolonged the treacherous events that had continued to steal the precious times from my development. In those stolen times, as I have just described, I had been a servant, a storekeeper, and a refugee in Aba, Lagos, and Kaduna, respectively, and a soldier in the Biafran Army.

These times were in stark contrast to the glamorous days of my childhood, even though I had no mother to cradle me in infancy. But I had a loving father, who guided and supported me generously throughout my childhood development and primary school education, which I proudly completed with great optimism and heightened expectations for a brighter future.

THE ROMANCES OF CHILDHOOD

The month of December 1960 was a lustrous landmark in my adolescent development and my journey to adulthood. It was the month I received the news that I had passed the Eastern Nigeria Ministry of Education First School Leaving Certificate Examination, Standard Six.

Actually, it was the precious moment that I had been anxiously waiting for, since I had taken the examination on Friday 25 November 1960. The examination exercise was centrally coordinated by the Ministry of Education and was held on the same day and at the same time for all primary school pupils in the entire Eastern Region of Nigeria. A common location was designated for a group of schools, and that was where the examination was taken. In our own case, it was the Methodist Primary Central School in Afugiri.

Several weeks following the examination, the results were distributed and posted on the announcement boards of the various district offices of the Ministry of Education in Umuahia. The pupils streamed in groups to those locations to obtain information about their performances in the examination.

I travelled to Umuahia with a group of friends. It was a journey of about six kilometres. This was not a big deal for us as youngsters. Besides, we were totally excited and anxious to know whether we had passed the examination or not. Two months earlier, we had paraded through the township, waving our green and white flags for the celebration of Nigeria's independence on 1 October 1960 from British rule. As school children, we were used to walking the distance every year for the celebration of the Empire Day on 24 May, the birthday of Queen Victoria, with parades and sporting competitions in the government field.

I was full of joy when I found my name on the announcement board. That meant that I had passed the examination. Of course, there were other pupils among us whose names did not appear on the list, meaning that they had failed the examination.

Walking and running, I returned home to the village to give the news of my success to my father. As other parents spent plenty of time comforting their children for their failure in the examination, I watched my father busily making preparations for a joyous Christmas and happy New Year celebrations for our family.

Throughout the Christmas and the New Year festivities, I observed my father's pride in my scholastic achievement. He was also very proud that he now had an adolescent son. People in the village did not believe that he could one day have a youngster of my calibre.

My father, Josaiah Ezenyiriume Azuru, began relatively very late in life to settle down in a home and establish his own family. His father, Azuru, was a nobiliary peasant farmer. He had many wives and slaves, plus a sizeable portion of farmland, which he had inherited from his father, Ugwuoji.

My father's mother, Ugwuezi, was the daughter of another nobiliary peasant farmer, Adiele, from Umunkaru, a neighbouring village. She had two sons and two daughters, of whom my father was the eldest. She named her younger daughter Mary because she was born in the churchyard of our village while she was going with her children to visit one of her sisters married in Nkata Alaike, a village in the Okaiuga community.

When the Europeans arrived in Ohuhu, they demanded that every village contribute a number of children to be educated at the missionary schools. But some parents in our village were initially skeptical of the plan. They were afraid that they might lose the vital support of their children to them at home and on the farm. So during the day, they hid their children in the bush, or deep in their homes. But my father's parents allowed him to go to school. He was one of the first sixteen children from our village to be educated at the missionary schools in Ohuhu.

My father married my mother, Elizabeth Egobeke, when he was already over forty years of age. He met my mother in Amaiyi Isukwuato, near Ovim, where her mother had come to live with her two daughters and a son. They were originally from Okposi in Afikpo.

Prior to my father's marriage with my mother, he worked for the Anglican Church as a priest. He carried out missionary work in various distant villages. Although he did not spent many years at school, he had received sufficient education to enable him to read and write.

In the meantime, my father's eldest half-brother died. He had been the only son living in the village to look after their father's properties, since my father and his junior brother were absent from home. My father interrupted his missionary work to return to the village, since he was the next in seniority to be in charge of the properties of their father according to the rules of primogeniture. By implication, he was obliged to embrace the predominating ancestral traditions of the people, and to give up the Christian religion, which was only beginning to take a competing foothold in the village.

As my father recounted, he was over and above himself with joy when, on a Wednesday in February at about four o'clock in the morning, he finally heard a baby crying in the back of our village house. It was the moment he had been waiting for all night and into the morning hours.

A group of women from the village, supervised by an experienced native midwife, surrounded my mother to assist her in her labour to deliver me onto a banana leaf over a bare, gravel floor. My mother was only eighteen years of age.

One of the women walked over to my father in the parlour to give him the news that my mother had given birth to a baby boy. On hearing that it was a boy, my father jumped up from his easy chair, took out his hunting gun from its resting place in one corner of the parlour, went out to the front of our house, and shot several times in the air to show his tremendous joy for the good news.

The villagers were prematurely awakened from their beds by my father's gunfire. As was customary, they rushed to our house to have a quick glimpse of the newborn baby and to congratulate my father and my mother.

Some of the people stopped over by our house on their way to the farms, or to fetch water from the river. Others came during the day to do the same. My father organized an impromptu party for all the guests and well-wishers. The women and children rallied round in our compound, singing and dancing to welcome the newborn baby into their midst.

My father called me Nkemakolam (let me not be in want

for what I desire) because he was happy to have his own son at last. My mother called me Chukwuemeka (God did well).

My senior cousin, Friday Umunna, later called me Smart. When I asked him why he had chosen the name for me, he said that, in his judgement, I was very special in my infancy, as I developed at a much faster rate in comparison to other infants in the village. I did not ask more questions, even though his explanation was not quite clear to me. But I assured myself that, for aught I knew, I must live up to the name! The name has been a big challenge for me ever since I adopted it officially.

To add to the long chain of my names, my baptism mother called me Benson when I was baptised in the Anglican Church in 1957. When everyone was finished, my full name was quite rich: Smart Nkemakolam Benson Chukwuemeka Josaiah Ezenyiriume Azuru nwa (the son of) Ukwuoji. However, for the sake of brevity, I decided to keep my name to Smart Nkemakolam Eze for all time.

The village into which I was born was called Akpahia Azumiri Umuezechiala. It was one of the villages that made up the Ohuhu community. In a historical perspective, the Ohuhu community must have undergone a significant change in its population some centuries ago.

Some parts of the population migrated across the major Ikwu River to settle on the vast empty land which stretched northwards up to Uzuakoli, Isuikwuato, and Okigwe regions. The ancestral father of my village, Ezechiala, must have taken advantage of the migration euphoria of the Ohuhu people of the time. He left his village Akpahia Okpuala (the land root of Akpahia) and crossed the major Ikwu River with his family, and settled down on the vast, empty land nearest to the water. It seemed he wanted to be close to his four brothers, whom he had left behind on the other side of the river. He named his village Akpahia Azumiri (Akpahia behind the water). His village stood on top of the hill looking over the Ikwu River. As he and his children were peasant farmers, they were able to take full advantage of the vegetation along the bank of the river as well as the dry land.

Their houses were built in compounds, each a cluster of buildings with a shared open space in the centre, encircled with a fence made of sticks and palm leaves and mats. Each compound was linked through an open passage to the village centre, which was used as an assembling place.

The village was expanded northwards in due course, as some parts of the community moved up the hill to live. They called the new section of the village New Dwelling and the original settlement area the Front of the Village.

A major road ran through the entire village from the hill down to the Ikwu River. A number of pathways led to the farm fields from the centre of the village. The village was embellished with different kinds of fruit plants and trees—mango tree, orange tree, umbrella tree, *udara* tree, banana tree, and many more. These trees served as natural air conditioners, shading the village and keeping it cool. They also protected the soil against erosion and provided food. It was a beautiful and homely little tropical village. The alley of the village was the major road to the Ikwu River; there were African oil bean trees planted on both sides of the road.

Most important, Ezechiala and his children planted an *iroko* tree and two silk cotton trees in the centre of their settlement. These trees were traditionally planted in the village squares of the communities throughout Ohuhu. The trees rapidly grew tall and wide, and played a crucial role in the spiritual and economic lives of the people. They were landmarks, symbols, and flags of the village that people could identify from far afield, and orient themselves appropriately. After Ezechiala's death, his two sons and their children added the word *Umuezechiala* (the children of Ezechiala) to the name of the village in honour of their father.

The marital harmony in my parental household did not last for a long period. When I was about four years old, the marriage of my parents broke up. One night, as my father was out of the house to attend a meeting, of which he was the secretary, my mother packed up her belongings, carried my little sister Anna Ada on her back, and left the house. My sister was only a little over two years of age.

My mother thought that I might not be able to sustain the long walk to her parents' home, given that I was just a little child, so she put me to bed in my father's bedroom and locked me up for safekeeping when I was asleep. She did not want me to run after her crying in the middle of the night, lest the people in the village know about her departure.

When my father returned from the meeting, he found me alone sleeping in the bedroom. It was immediately clear to him that my mother must have gone back to her parents. They had been having prolonged disagreements with each other, and my mother had reached the point of no return. Reconciliation between them was no longer feasible. My sister was eventually returned to my father after several months of prolonged legal battling. But the marriage between my mother and my father could not be repaired any more. They were permanently divorced from each other.

Taking care of two little children was not so easy for my father. But he was surrounded by a number of close family relations, who readily offered to help him in the difficult situation.

I was barely six years of age when my father's brother Aaron Nnabugwu took me away from the village to Port Harcourt to live with him and his wife. They had a little child of about two years of age. My uncle worked as a ship labourer in the Port Harcourt harbour, and his wife was a market woman, trading in fruits and vegetables at the market in Diob Mile 3, one of the notorious districts of the town.

As I later experienced, she was heartless and cruel to me. For, actually, I had come to live with them and serve them as a houseboy. She forced me to perform duties in the household, which were utterly impossible for a little child of my age. The drudgery included going to draw water from the public well, cradling her little child, carrying heavy loads to the market for her, and so on.

My uncle seemed not to be aware of her maltreatment of me, since he was working on a ship at the harbour during the day. Even when he was off duty and stayed at home, the other tenants could not talk to him about his wife's malicious treatment of his little nephew because he was an introvert who avoided contact with the people in the yard at all cost.

Each day, whenever I had the opportunity, I would stroll off to a nearby school to watch the pupils in action. I was particularly fascinated by their uniforms, exercises on the playground, and classroom environment, which I observed from a distance. My uncle's wife, at times, did not know where I was because sometimes I missed my way and did not return home for many hours. One day, my uncle was at work and his wife was at the market with her little child. I had wandered off to the nearby school for my usual observations. On that day, my father had travelled by train from Umuahia to visit my uncle and his family and to apprise himself of my condition. When he arrived at the house, the people in the yard briefed my father thoroughly about my miserable living conditions in his brother's household. When my uncle's wife returned from the market in the evening without me, it was clear to my father that I had gone missing again. He immediately started off to the market and to the nearby school in search of me. He finally found me in a carpenter's shop, totally confused, hungry, emaciated, and very frail.

He carried me on his shoulders and walked back to the home of my uncle and his wife. They had serious discussions throughout the evening and into the night when my uncle returned from work.

My father was very upset and highly disappointed with my uncle and his wife, because he did not find any justification for their inhumane treatment of his six-year-old child. He did not want me to be subjected to such hardship and miserable condition anymore by them in their household.

The following day, very early in the morning, my father carried me on his shoulders and walked straight to the Port Harcourt Railway Station. We took the suburban train and travelled home to Umuahia.

Back in our village, in the following months, my father was primarily concerned with the task of repairing my devastated and very poor health, which had been caused by the inhumane treatment of my uncle and his wife, and my living in a slum and unhygienic environment in Port Harcourt. My malnourished condition was not an insoluble problem for my father, since he had plenty of food in the house, and his family relations were ready to step in and help with my feeding. But I was suffering from another condition as well, and he considered it necessary to confront these two health condition problems of mine headlong concurrently, as they were both the culprits for my horrible condition. Therefore, he took me to the dispensary near our village, where the dispenser, who was a white man, prescribed very effective doses of castor oil, which my father administered to me at home. It was a very powerful purgative, which effectively freed me from all the internal parasites that I had contracted in Port Harcourt.

Finally, I was a happy child again, and in excellent health. As I was nearing eight years of age, my father approached his uncle, Ememandu Adiele, and his wife, Mmazue, for their support with my long-overdue schooling; it was usual for children to be sent to school at the age of six.

My great uncle and his wife lived in a nearby village called Umunkaru, which was only a twenty-minute walk from our village. They had two grown-up children of their own, Daniel Iroakazi and his sister, Ada Ememandu. They took me from my father to live with them as the third child in the family.

When I arrived in Umunkaru to live with my great uncle and his wife, I found the environment relatively similar to that of my village. The people lived in compounds, which were broadly spread out. The familiar iroko trees, the silk cotton trees, and the various fruit trees were planted all over the village.

The village was split into upper and lower sections, connected together by an alley of African oil bean trees. Each section had a village square, which was centrally located.

At the intersection on the upper section of the village, the first road led to my village, the second to the Ikwu River and a neighbouring village, the third to the Umuahia/Uzuakoli main road and the primary school, the fourth was the alley connecting the two sections of the village and down to the Ama Stream, the Orie Amaenyi market, and other neighbouring villages. I felt so much at home, both in the household of my great uncle and his wife and in the whole environment around me.

In January 1953, my great uncle, Ememandu, went with me to the Orie Amaenyi Methodist Primary Central School, for me to be registered as a pupil. The school was centrally located on the Umuahia/Uzuakoli main road at Amauhie and Umuyota for the convenience of the group of the villages hosting it. The name of the school, Orie Amaenyi, was derived from the community market day of these villages.

For the intelligence and the physical maturity tests, I raised my hand over my head and reached my ear on the other side, and responded to some logical questions that were put to me. I passed these tests easily, and was admitted to the school. I was so happy and excited that, at last, I could go to school to fulfil my childhood ambition, which my uncle and his wife had maliciously denied me in Port Harcourt.

The compound of the Orie Amaenyi Methodist Primary Central School covered a large area of land which stretched from the Umuahia/Uzuakoli main road deep into the farm fields beyond. It was laid out in a rectangular shape, and fenced all around with bamboo sticks and flower hedges. There were two big gates on the side of the fence to the main road, and a smaller gate in the middle of the right side of the fence for the traffic of the pupils from the villages behind. There was a big football field, a netball field, and several lawns with footpaths and beautiful flowerbeds on both sides.

As one entered through the first gate on the main road into the school compound, the houses for the teachers were on the left—three groups of houses, standing in a straight line to one another, and facing the netball field, the football field, and the school buildings.

The first group of houses was for the head master, the second was for the assistant head master, and the third was for the rest of the teachers. The houses were separated from each other by big lawns. There was a big farm behind each house where the teachers could grow essential foods for their individual consumption.

There were three buildings for the classrooms, which stood in an L-formation facing the assembling ground. One of them was a mud-thatched house, and had been built more recently. The other two had been built with concrete blocks much earlier in the development of the school.

The big school farm and the pit latrine facilities were behind the buildings. All over the premises there were cashew trees, mango trees, whistle trees, fir trees, palm trees, guava trees, umbrella trees, and so on, all of which kept the school pleasantly cool and beautiful at all times.

The pupils from the area where we lived entered the school compound through the first gate from the main road. I was extremely excited and very proud when I entered the school compound through that gate for the first time. I was neatly dressed in my new school uniform and carried my wooden slate and chalk and reading textbooks in my school bag.

We went to school from Monday through Friday. The school bell was persistently rung twice every morning at an interval of thirty minutes. It was a big bell, which hung on a tall tree in the school compound, so that the pupils could hear it ringing from far afield in the villages.

When the bell rang the second and final time at eight o'clock, the three main gates were automatically closed to signal the beginning of the school programme for the day. This insured that the pupils who arrived late could not enter the school compound and disturb the proceedings of the early morning rituals on the assembling ground.

At the ringing of the final bell, we all rushed to the assembling ground in front of the school buildings, and filed in to our respective classes like troops on a military parade. On rainy days, the early morning rituals were performed in the school hall.

The teachers and the head master stood in front of the lines of the pupils as the early morning rituals were performed, which involved singing songs from the hymn book and saying prayers. The head master and the teachers made general announcements on the school's programmes for the day.

Our head master, who was recognizable by the whip he always carried under his arm, distributed the appropriate punishments to the pupils who had offended the school rules.

These pupils were given a couple of the lashes of the whip. Some might also be retained after the school hours to perform punishment duties. Punishable offences included arriving late at school in the morning, being absent from school duties, and even not turning up for the football and netball games.

At the end of the morning assembly, since our school did not have a music band of its own, we all matched proudly into our respective classrooms singing the last hymn of the ritual proceedings. The main school gates were then opened for the pupils who came late to enter the compound and join their peers in the classrooms.

In carrying out our duties at school, we were not only organized into class levels but also into groups, or 'houses', which were named after renowned national patriots of the period: the Azikiwe House, the Crowder House, the Ojike House, and the Ibiam House. Each group had a prefect at its head and a teacher in an advisory position to support the group.

A number of points were calculated and awarded to the individual groups for their performances in the various duties of the school, such as working on the farm, cutting the lawns, mending the fences, sweeping the paths, maintaining the flower beds, playing football and netball games, working in the teachers' quarters, and so on.

At the end of the year, the flag of the group that scored the highest points on aggregate was hoisted over the assembling ground, where it flew and fluttered until that group was beaten in the performance evaluation of the school duties by another.

Virtue, industry, and discipline were the uppermost principles on the agenda of our school as a missionary institution. It was an eight-year (eight classes) primary school programme. It began with Infant One and Infant Two, and then went on to Standard One through Standard Six.

In Infant One, we learned to write texts and draw pictures on a wooden slate with chalk in different colours; we had printed books for reading and comprehension. In Infant Two, we were introduced to writing texts and drawing pictures on a paper with ink and pen, pencil, and crayon. The pen consisted of a holder and a nib as a unit, and had to be frequently dipped into the inkpot for refilling. We were later permitted, in the upper classes, to also use fountain pens for writing texts.

The curriculum of the school covered arithmetic, nature study, geography, history, hygiene, physical training, drawing, handiwork, singing, English, Igbo, religious knowledge, and farming. Among these subjects, arithmetic was the one that I favoured most, and I was extremely strong in it right from my first day at school. For example, already in my second year at school in Infant Two, I was called up one morning by the teacher of the pupils in Standard Four to help resolve an arithmetical calculation in his class. None of the pupils in the class had been able to resolve the calculation. The teacher stood me on a high chair so that I could write comfortably on the blackboard. I took the chalk and wrote the arithmetical procedure neatly and sequentially on the blackboard while the teacher and his pupils watched me in action. I then made the arithmetical calculations and arrived at the correct result.

The arithmetical problem was resolved. The pupils of the class spontaneously applauded for me. They were genuinely astounded by my performance. They could not imagine how the little boy from Infant Two was able to resolve the arithmetical calculation that had troubled their entire class. The teacher made them loudly clap hands repeatedly for me. As I returned to my classroom in Infant Two, I hoped that the pupils in Standard Four did not feel depressed or humiliated by my performance in their classroom. I had only done the calculations correctly because I knew how.

However, with all humility, the event had lifted me up beyond the classroom of the pupils of Standard four, and made me popular in the entire school. Nkemakolam Eze, the little boy in Infant Two, was now known by everyone in the school, especially the teachers and the head master.

In 1955, I interrupted my education at the Orie Amaenyi Methodist Primary central School, even though I had successfully passed the Infant Two final examination to advance to Standard One. However, I could not be admitted to the new class, because the maximum number of pupils required in Standard One for that year had been met with children from the seven villages sponsoring the school. The inhabitants of these villages were levied a substantial amount of money, which they contributed regularly to the building fund of the school. As a consequence, their children were given priority for admission to and retention at the school. As I was not a child born in any of the sponsoring villages, and my father was not a contributor to the building fund, I could not be retained at the school to read Standard One.

It was an unfortunate circumstance, which momentarily seemed to be beyond the control of my teacher, our head master, my father, and my great uncle. However, I was not alone in this uncomfortable situation, because there were also three other pupils who could not be retained at the school in that year.

But our head master soon helped us to obtain admission at the Ubani Ibeku Local Development Primary School, which was eight kilometres away from Orie Amaenyi. The school had presently only Infant One, Infant Two, Standard One, and Standard Two, as it was still being developed by the local community. Usually, after four years at the school, pupils continued their education at the primary schools in Orie Amaenyi or Afugiri. It was that mutual cooperation between the missionary schools in the area that facilitated the efforts of our head master to have us transferred temporarily to the new school.

The somewhat long distance from our villages to the Ubani Ibeku Local Development Primary school did not pose any insurmountable problems to us, given that we were three boys and one girl who unconditionally supported one another. We had two alternative ways to get to the school. However, each of the routes had its weak and strong points. We walked to our new school either along the Umuahia-Uzuakoli main road, which was not yet tarred, or along the bush road, as a shortcut.

Our daily journeys to the school always began at six o'clock in the morning from our central meeting point in the village. This meant that we had to wake up much earlier to wash our bodies and have a quick breakfast, to dress up in our uniforms, and be ready in time for the eight-kilometres journey. We walked and ran so as to be at the school by eight o'clock when the school programmes began for the day.

To get to the school by either route, we crossed three streams. On the Umuahia-Uzuakoli main road, bridges and culverts spanned the streams. But on the bush road, the neighbouring farmers had improvised long trunks of trees to serve as bridges that they used when they travelled to their farms and to the neighbouring villages. In the rainy season, those streams overflowed their banks and flooded the surrounding farms. The long trunks of trees we had once walked over disappeared completely from sight. In that circumstance, we resorted to one of our childhood skills, which proved to be practical and very effective, to overcome the challenge. We removed our uniforms and tied them over our heads, then swam and walked across the waters to the dry land on the other side.

To protect ourselves from the falling rain, we held over our head a big banana or plantain leaf, which we cut from the tree. We occasionally saw pythons and cobras crossing from one side of the bush pathways to the other in a very close distance. We protected ourselves from them by running away as fast as we could. We also hurried away from any spot along the bush pathways where we detected the intense fresh smells of wild cats.

Our school day was extremely long, as it lasted from dawn to dusk. If we were given assignments to perform at home, we stayed behind to complete them at the end of the school day. We took our school bags home with us only on Fridays so we could study over the weekend at home.

We preferred to use the Umuahia-Uzuakoli main road for our return journeys from school, as we always had a lot of fun walking and running along the road. Most important, we had plenty of time for ourselves, and were not under pressure whatsoever to get home. There were plenty of fruit trees along the way. We climbed them and plucked bananas, oranges, pineapples, mangoes, pawpaws, and palm fruits and ate until our stomachs were satisfied. We always had our pocket knives with us ready for action. The owners did not mind that hungry school children had eaten of their fruit trees. Besides, the amount of fruit that we consumed in total was relatively insignificant compared to the bearings on the trees. If we were thirsty, we simply walked down to the nearest stream and drank our fill.

We always arrived home shortly before sunset, except when we occasionally encountered the herdsmen from the north of the country with their cattle on the Umuahia-Uzuakoli main road. They wandered for several days with their cattle, grazing them along the way, and heading towards the Umuahia township, where they sold them to the slaughterhouses. Sometimes, the herds numbered over fifty cows. They would block the entire road, and we would be unable to overtake them. We were compelled to walk slowly behind the herdsmen and their cattle for a long while at a respectable distance until they reached the stream where they left the road so the cows could drink. Occasionally, a lorry would approach, and the herdsmen would steer the cows off the road to create space for the vehicle to pass. Then we would seize the opportunity to overtake the herdsmen and their cattle on the spot without wasting any more time.

While I was at school, my great uncle, Ememandu Adiele, died. His daughter, Ada Ememandu, had married and moved with her husband to another village. His son, Daniel Iroakazi Ememandu, had gone to Kaduna, in the Northern Region, in search of a job after he completed his primary education.

I promptly moved into my cousin's room in the house, and furnished it in a manner to suit my boyish taste. For fun, I wired my room electrically with used radio batteries and electric bulbs, which I collected from the refuse dumps in the Umuahia township. I carefully opened the electric bulbs and inserted new and small torch lamps into them to illuminate my entire room. I had so many of those lamps all over my room that I could quietly and peacefully read and study at night.

I was the only child at home living with my great uncle's wife, Mmazue Ememandu Adiele. She was happy to have me around to keep her company; otherwise she would have been lonely in the house. Besides, I was now grown up enough to help her in those household activities which a child of my age could perform. I was grateful living with her, as she cared for me as a mother would care for her own.

The most common activity of children in the household of their parents was fetching water from the stream and firewood from the bush. In the case of water supply, the village of my great uncle was not advantageously located. Especially because, in the dry season, the Ama Stream, the nearest source of water supply for the villagers, dried up completely. The people were compelled to stride all the way to the main Ikwu River to fetch water several times in a day, which was approximately a two-kilometre journey in either direction. It was always a great relief for Mmazue that I could help her with these activities, which were essential for our living.

Like most women in the community, Mmazue was also a pottery maker, from which she made some extra money for our livelihood. To support her in the business, I collected the clay material from distant locations, where it was dug out from the pits and sold to buyers. At home, I delightedly watched as she mixed the clay with fine sand and water, and then thrashed and mollified it to produce beautiful pots of different shapes and decorations. I usually helped to keep an eye on the pots, bringing them out to the sun to dry. Once the pots were sufficiently dried, we made a huge fire in a free place in the village centre and burned them to harden them. Thereafter, the pots were ready for sale. We sold some on the spot or at our home, and others we carried to the markets.

While I lived with Mmazue, communications between my father and me were not interrupted in any way. Because of the negligible distance between Umunkaru and Akpahia Azumiri, I visited my father frequently whenever I wanted to do so, and had the necessary time available to me. Sometimes, I went to stay with my father for a couple of days during the school holidays. And sometimes I spent some days with my aunt Mary in Umuaram, a village very close to Umunkaru, and went to school from there.

My aunt Mary was married to Ukachi, a nobiliary peasant

farmer. He had many wives and many children. But my aunt had only two boys, Uju and Ihueze, who were almost of my age. Whenever I stayed with her, I went together with them to the Orie Amaenyi Methodist Central Primary School.

The proximity of the three villages to one another was especially auspicious for my childhood development. Although my principal dwelling place was at my great uncle's house in Umunkaru, I could visit or stay with my father or my aunt Mary whenever I wanted to do so.

Meanwhile, my father remarried a young woman from Alai, a distant village north of Umuahia. She came to my father's house with a young child from her previous marriage. She was a very strong woman, hard-working, and understood everything about farming. She was from a rich farmer's family. My father told me that her personality was totally the opposite to that of my mother, who was not very fond of farming. However, right from the outset, my sister and I could not get on well with our stepmother. We quarrelled most of the time with her because of the preferential treatment that she gave to her daughter.

Our father did not listen to us whenever we complained to him about our stepmother's unfair treatment of us. He always tended to be on the side of his wife and her daughter. My sister and I detested that attitude of our father because it continuously reminded us of the absence of our own mother in the house.

We envied other children when we saw how their mothers were treating them, and we imagined what it would be like to experience that sort of mother-and-child relationship. Moreover, the people in the village, out of pity and sympathy, always treated us like orphans, which even made us feel more disadvantaged, neglected, and abandoned.

One of the things I very much enjoyed in the village were the children's nocturnal plays, whether I was staying with my aunt, my great uncle's wife, or my father. Before going to sleep after the evening meal, in the light of the full moon, the children gathered in the centre of the compound, sitting on the mats laid out in a half-moon format around a mother, an aunt, or an older sister who told the children many fairy tales. The children listened carefully to the stories, at the end of which they were asked questions about what they had learned from the story. The fairy tales were packed full of wisdom on everyday life experiences. Thereafter, the children stood up and cheerfully ran into the village square to play a hide-and-find game before going back to their respective homes to sleep for the night.

I was especially fascinated by the story about the udara, a deciduous fruit which was highly desired by children. I perfectly identified its similarity to my own life experience. During the udara season, no mother ever went to the market and returned without buying it for her children at home:

> Once upon a time, a little girl lived in a small village with her stepmother and her father. The stepmother had a little son. Whenever she went to the market, she bought plenty of udara for her son and herself. When she returned from the market, she called her son to her room and they ate all of the fruits while the little girl watched sadly. The stepmother gave none of the fruits to the poor little girl.
>
> But the udara had a very beautiful seed, which was not edible like the flesh. It was taken out from the flesh and discarded carelessly all over the environment. The little girl went about collecting the seeds to

play with like all the other children in the village.

One day, the little girl suddenly had a marvellous idea: she went behind her village house, dug a small hole in the earth, and planted one of her udara seeds in the soil. She went regularly to water her udara seed with a watering can, since the soil was constantly dried up from the sun.

The little girl thought out a beautiful song, which she sang while dancing and watering her udara seed. She talked to her udara in that song, in which she expressed her eight wishes in the form of commands.

The little girl followed each of her wishes with a refrain in which she passionately complained that her father's wife always bought udara from the market, ate all of it, and gave none to the child who had no mother of her own. She considered herself to be an orphan because her father never intervened on the matter on her behalf. But, she recognized that this world was a transit, from which everyone must go one day.

In the first song, the little girl asked her udara seed to germinate. The udara seed sprouted immediately from the earth. The little girl could not believe her eyes. She exclaimed joyfully, 'It works! My udara can listen to me. It can obey me to fulfil my many wishes!'

As the little girl watered the udara plant, she sang the second song and asked her udara seedling to grow to a big tree. Her wish was fulfilled. A huge udara tree now stood behind her village house. The little girl looked up and was so happy as she danced and watered the huge udara tree at its foot.

In the third song, the little girl wished the udara tree to bear plenty of fruit. All of a sudden, there were so many fruits all over the branches of the tree. The little girl danced jubilantly and watered more intensively around the foot of the udara tree. She looked up to the tree and observed that the fruits were still too tiny and vulnerable.

In the fourth song, the little girl wished that the fruits of her udara tree would get bigger, stronger, and juicier. As she danced and watered her udara tree, she saw that all its branches were heavily laden with big, strong, and juicy fruits. The little girl was very pleased at the sight. But she recognized that the fruits were still sour and were not delicious enough to be eaten yet.

As the little girl danced and watered the udaraa tree, she wished in the fifth song that those big, strong, and juicy fruits would ripen. She was pleased that her wish was swiftly fulfilled and that many of the fruits were sufficiently ripe. The birds were sitting, fluttering, and singing on the branches of the tree. The bees were flying in and out of the tree in a celebrative mood.

The little girl saw all that and was very satisfied. She now had her own udara, which belonged to her alone. She could not stop dancing as she watered the tree, and could no longer wait to taste the udara fruit. But her udara tree had grown so high, and she was still a little girl. She could not climb the high tree to pluck one of the fruits.

In the sixth song, the little girl asked the udara tree to let one of its fruits fall down to the earth for her. The tree obliged her and let one of its fruits fall to the earth for the little girl. She quickly picked up the fruit from the ground and washed it perfectly clean with the water from her watering can.

She carefully bit a small piece of the fruit, and kept in her mouth for a little while. Then, she said, 'Oh, this is udara, and this is how it tastes!' When she finished eating the fruit, she looked up to the tree and talked to it saying, 'Look, my udara tree, I have another very special wish.'

The udara tree replied, 'Yes, but what is it?' The little girl said, 'I am going for a short walk in the forest. If anyone comes to pluck your fruits, send one of your leaves to me wherever I am so that I can rush home immediately!' The udara tree replied, 'Yes, your wish shall always be fulfilled.'

The little girl had barely arrived in the forest for her walk when she suddenly saw the leaf of an udara tree falling in front of her. It landed on her toes. She picked it up, looked at it, and smelled it. She recognized it right away. It was a leaf from her very own tree. She interrupted her walk immediately, turned round, and ran back home as fast as she possibly could.

As soon as she arrived home, she went straight to her udara tree. Whom did she see there on top of the tree? It was her half-brother. The little boy could not resist the temptations of the inviting sight and the smell of the ripe, juicy fruits behind the house. He had climbed up into the tree to pluck some of the fruits to eat.

But that was too much for the little girl to tolerate. She was so upset and very angry at the sight of her half-brother on her udara tree. She sang the seventh of her habitual songs as fast as she could, almost without breathing, in which she wished the udara tree to quickly grow higher.

The more she sang, the higher the tree grew. The little boy remained in the tree and soon he vanished into the clouds. Nothing of the boy could be seen from the ground anymore. All that could be seen was the long trunk of the tree stretching up into the clouds in the sky.

Pretty soon, the mother of the little boy returned from the market. But before she reached their home, the people in the village told her about the fate of her son. She cried passionately and was heartbroken. She was terrified and worried about her son.

The father of the little girl returned home from the farm. The people in the village informed him about the tragedy of his son. The father felt very anxious and apprehensive about his little boy.

When the father finally arrived at the

scene, he pleaded passionately to the little girl to tell her udara tree to bring the boy down to earth. He knew that the tree always obeyed the little girl. He promised that, if she made it happen, he would divide all his possessions into three parts. He pledged to give two-thirds of them to the little girl. The little girl was not quite convinced by her father's promises, but she wanted to give him the benefit of the doubt.

She looked up to the clouds in the sky, lowered her voice, and gently sang the eighth song, in which she wished her Udara tree to come down slowly to the earth. The spectators, including the man and his wife, were all excited as they stood with their eyes tightly fixed to the clouds in the sky. They watched as the tree began to lower itself gradually.

The more the little girl sang her song, the more slowly the udara tree came down to the earth with the little boy until it reached its normal height. The father hurriedly brought his son down from the tree. As he promised, he immediately divided all his possessions into three parts and gave two-thirds of them to the little girl.

The mother and the little boy, and the little girl and their father embraced one another and bowed to the spectators from the village who had gathered to bear witness to the event. Holding hands and smiling, they walked back to their village house,

where they lived together happily. If they did
not die, they would be alive today.

At the end of the story, the children would be asked some contextual questions about the story. Some of the questions might be, Was the stepmother nice to the little girl? Did the father keep his promise? Was the little girl nice to the udara tree? Was the udara tree nice to the little girl?

The children, who were little boys and little girls, competed with one another in their answers to the questions. Then they would thank the storyteller and ran out happily to the village square for the hide-and-find game in the full bright moonlight.

The Udara Tree	Osisi Udara

1. My udara sprout, right,
Sprout, sprout, sprout, right.

Refrain:
My father's wife, right,
Bought udara from the market, right,
Ate all of it, right,
Giving none to a motherless child,
A fatherless, motherless child,
This world is a transit, right,
One day one must go, right.

2. My udara grow, right,
Grow, grow, grow, right.

3. My udara fruit, right,
Fruit, fruit, fruit, right.

4. My udara big, right,
Bigger, bigger, bigger, right.

5. My udara ripe, right,
Ripe, ripe, ripe, right.

6. My udara fall, right,
Fall, fall, fall, right.

7. My udara high, right,
Higher, higher, higher, right.

8. My udara down, right,
Down, down, down, right.

---

1. Udara mu puo, nda,
Puo, puo, puo, nda.

Refrain:
Nwunye nna mu, nda,
Zuta udara na'ahia, nda,
Ra, ra, racha, nda,
Rachapu nwa enwe nne,
Nwa enwe nna, nwa enwe nne,
Eluwa obu olili, nda,
Onye nocha olaba, nda.

2. Udara mu to, nda,
To, to, to, nda.

3. Udara mu mia, nda,
Mia, mia, mia, nda.

4. Udara mu ka, nda,
Ka, ka, ka, nda.

5. Udara mu cha, nda,
Cha, cha, cha, nda.

6. Udara mu da, nda,
Da, da, da, nda.

7. Udara mu tia, nda,
Tia, tia, tia, nda.

8. Udara mu suo, nda,
Suo, suo, suo, nda.

One night, as the hide-and-find game was over in the village centre, we children began running back to our homes to sleep. But some dark clouds began to deny the moon its full brightness. The moon intermittently became dim in the sky, and gradually darkened the village. I was afraid to go back home alone. Onyebuchi, a good friend of mine, offered to escort me to my house. When we reached the gate of my house, the sky got even darker. He then became afraid of going back to his house alone. Our two compounds were about 300 metres apart. I volunteered to escort him back to his house.

By the time we reached the gate of his compound, the moon was scarcely visible in the sky. Again, I was afraid to go back to my house alone. Instinctively, we struck a childhood deal. Together we walked to a point halfway between our houses. Then we stopped, and each of us began running in the direction of our respective home. Running as fast as we could, we halloed and responded at intervals to each other's call. We only stopped those calls when we finally arrived at the gates of our respective compounds. I opened the gate quietly in order not to wake up my great uncle's wife, and went straight to sleep. I was very happy to be home and safe in my bed at last after all those exciting nocturnal entertainments.

In 1957, I left the Ubani Ibeku Local Development Methodist Primary School after completing the Standard Two, and I returned back to the Orie Amaenyi Methodist Central Primary School to continue my education at the Standard Three level. Although I enjoyed my entire period at the Ubani Ibeku school, I was nonetheless happy to be relieved from the early morning and late evening journeys to and from the school.

When I arrived at the Orie Amaenyi Methodist Central

Primary School, I met my previous classmates from the Infant Two, who were also now in the Standard Three. Most of the teachers remembered me, especially the head master, who was very pleased to have me back in his school.

I was pleasantly surprised that my popularity had not diminished despite my two years of absence from the school. My teachers were all enthusiastic about my performance, both in and outside the classroom. The individual teachers appointed me a class monitor every year from Standard Three until Standard Six, which was my final year at the school. It was a prestigious position, for which I was constantly envied by many of the other pupils. As a class monitor, my duties were to help keep my fellow pupils in line during the school day, help my teacher to maintain our classroom in a neat and well organized manner, and to assist our teacher with special projects.

Sometimes I was asked to help set up our classroom just as our teacher wanted it, such as moving the chairs and the desks as required. Every morning, I came in to school earlier than the other students to bring our teacher's stool and the schoolbooks from his or her house to the classroom; then I carried them back at the end of the day.

Sometimes, I swept the classroom and wiped the blackboard, the desks, and the chairs with a duster or a rag. I made sure that the supply of chalk in different colours was sufficiently available on our teacher's desk, and there was always a bundle of whips in the teacher's corner for eventual disciplinary measures in the classroom. Our female teacher in Standard Five, who was also our assistant head mistress, sometimes made me stay behind in her house after the schools hours to help her in correcting the assignments of my fellow pupils.

On Fridays at the end of the school hours, I went to the various classrooms and collected the syllabus books, the attendance registers, and other administrative books from the individual teachers for inspection and correction over the weekend by our head master, who was also our teacher in Standard Six. On Monday mornings, I returned those books again to all the teachers in their classrooms.

There was always a flurry of activity whenever the district education officer from the Ministry of Education came to our school for the periodic inspections. Our head master, the teachers, and the pupils would be excited, and worked hard to keep the whole premises clean, and the school and the administrative books in perfect order. As the class monitor, I gave our head master the necessary support before the arrival of the district education officer by providing him reports on the condition of the classrooms, and the entire school premises, including the pit latrine facilities and the school farm.

My duties as a class monitor did not prevent me from taking part in a variety of extra curricula activities. I enjoyed football tremendously, which I played very well for our school. In the testimonial accompanying my First School Leaving Certificate, our games master commented about me, 'He was useful to the school as a junior footballer.'

I was also one of the Boys' Brigade of our school. We were very enthusiastic about community work in the neighbourhood. From time to time, singing our brigade songs and carrying our hoes, machetes, buckets, and other tools, we would march into the surrounding villages to clean up the environment and help the elderly people in their homes and farms. We cut the mats from the palm trees, knitted them, and replaced the old ones on the roofs of the houses, and mended the mudded walls.

Farming was one of the subjects on our school curriculum. But the method that we used at school was slightly different from the system traditionally applied by the peasant farmers in the village. At school, farming began for us in November, and we cultivated the same field every year. We dug the soil in ridges and planted the crops. We did not cut and burn the trees and plants, and dump them elsewhere in the field. Instead, we cut the grass, the plants, and leaves from the trees and laid them between the ridges where they would be transformed into high-quality compost, which was great nourishment for the soil. Our moderate use of industrial fertilizers also helped to increase the fertility of the soil.

Every year, our school farm yielded plenty of high-quality crops, even to the admiration of the peasant farmers in the village. At harvesting time, we organized a special 'open door' day when we invited our parents and other people from the villages to purchase the farm products of our school. The pupils—both boys and girls—entertained the guests with folk songs and folk dances. In the meantime, our parents and other guests from the villages bought the farm products enthusiastically.

I was now a grown-up boy and was able to help my father and my great uncle's wife on their farms. As I mentioned, the traditional method of farming in the village differed slightly from the one that we practised at school. At the village level, the preparation for the work on the farm traditionally began in January at the climax of the Hamatan season. The Hamatan, also known as Harmattan, is a dry and dusty West African trade wind that blows across the Sahara Desert into the Gulf of Guinea. It usually begins at the end of November and ends in the middle of March, and marks the beginning of the dry season. On its passage through the desert, it picks up fine particles of dust. The temperature falls drastically between twenty-five and even down to eleven degrees Celsius in the mornings, evenings, and nights. We would shiver with cold at those times, sitting, squatting, or standing around open fires in the compounds and in the village centre, wearing woollen jackets and mufflers, to keep off the cold before embarking on any activities of the day. But, during the day, when the temperature could rise up to, and even above 50 degrees centigrade, my father and I, like the other peasant farmers in the village, took full advantage of the Hamatan season to cut, burn, and clear the fields for cultivating our three crops—yams, cocoyams, and cassavas—which began before the beginning of the rainy season in the middle of March. My father and I laboriously dug big, high mounds for planting the yams, and smaller and lower ones for the cocoyams and cassavas. We also dug trenches in some fields for planting the yams and the cassavas.

The cassava crop was planted in various locations in any of the three kinds of fields, whereas the yam and the cocoyam crops were planted only in their designated fields. But our major planting field was the yam farm, primarily managed by my father according to the farming tradition of our land.

Before planting the yams, my father cut each one into several setts. Each of the yam setts carried parts of the yam tuber. He would open the mound in the centre and carefully sow the yam. As he covered the yam, he would insert folded palm tree leaves into the hole and arrange them over the yam tuber as shade to protect it from the sun.

As gradually more rain fell, the yam plants appeared and grew quickly. It was the appropriate time to construct the stakes for the vines in the yam fields. My father and I carried hundreds of stout sticks and bamboos to our various fields. We sharpened the end of each one of the stakes so they could be driven into the ground. In the yam fields, the vines from three mounds were routinely connected to a stake in their centre. We would work from dawn to dusk, tying long ropes between the top of the posts and the young plants, training the yam vines and the tendrils to climb up in the desired direction. The ropes were traditionally made of palm tree materials.

After my father and I had completed the part of the farm work for which men were traditionally responsible, my father's wife planted other crops around the middle body of the mounds. Some of the crops included melons, pumpkins, and even cassava sticks.

Around the foot of the mounds, she planted other crops like the maize, garden eggplant, peppers, and okra. She also planted cassava and other crops in the trenches which I had dug wherever there was extra space available in the yam field.

The other two farm fields were totally under the control of my father's wife. But I dug the mounds and the trenches for her to plant cocoyams, cassavas, maize, okra, garden eggs, pepper plants, pumpkins, melons, and other crops. I also helped her in weeding all three of our fields, even though weeding was traditionally the labour for the female members of the household.

June, July, and August were the harvesting period for many of the crops. Food was in abundance in my father's house and in my great uncle's house. At last, we were happy to reap the fruits of our hard labour in the farm fields during the planting season.

We were excited when my father returned from the farm with the first harvest of the new yam. In this first phase of the harvesting process, my father would very carefully dig the mound open to reach the new yam. He would then cut off the greater part of it, leaving the rest with the yam tuber. My father did not wait until the final harvesting in November before he brought home yams to feed his family. In the second and the final phase of the harvesting process, my father harvested all the yams in the fields at once, including those he had cut in the first phase. He then would dig around the mounds to loosen the yam tubers from the soil, carefully lift them, and cut the yam vines with the corm attached to the tubers. We would gather the yams in the fields, carry them to the stream for washing, and bring them home to the barn for storage.

Like everyone else in the village, my father had only one yam barn on our compound. Of all the yams stored in our yam barn, he used 75 per cent for our food consumption until the next harvesting period, and 25 per cent for the next planting season.

But in the past, the farmers stored their harvested yams in two distinct locations in our village. They kept some of the yams in the barns on the compounds, and others in the general yam barn, as was done in all the neighbouring villages. The general yam barn of our village once stood in a mutually agreed upon location, which was slightly away from the compounds. Space in the barn was allocated to every farmer for storing his yams.

The yams in the barns on the compounds were exclusively meant for food, whereas those in the general barn were partly used as seeds for the next planting season, or were sold for money at the markets.

But, as I was growing up, I observed only the relics of the general yam barn of our village. It must have been abandoned some four or five decades previously. The only concrete evidence of its existence was the stout sticks, the bamboos, and the ropes with which the yams had once been tied together in the various divisions of the barn. They were all presently dilapidated, including the fence that was also constructed of stout sticks, bamboos, and other palm tree materials to protect the yams from the rodents and from unauthorised persons.

The advent of the British colonial administration at the

end of the previous century was a crucial turning point in the lives of the people in the villages, including mine. The administration had embarked on constructing townships, roads, railways, and harbours. The administration also established post offices, police and military forces, educational institutions, hospitals, and churches all over the land. It was compelled to draw from the citizens the manpower that it badly needed to develop and administer these infrastructure programmes. These programmes provided the citizens opportunities for employment, which were hitherto unheard off. The peasant farmers, including those from my village, were quickly lured to them. More and more farmers left the village and went to the townships to work for the white man. They popularly called it 'white man's job' in order to distinguish it clearly from their own work on the farm. They were happy, satisfied, and proud because the jobs were very lucrative in comparison to working on their farms, which was hard, arduous, and laborious, and offered them very low remuneration.

I counted approximately forty-five households in my little village when I was growing up. Each household had an average of six members, and was led by an adult male member. Later, I observed that over half of the adult male population had moved from the village to the townships in search of the 'white man's job'. Only the very old men and women stayed behind in the village to work on the farms. Some of the old women were on their own, as they were widows, and their young sons, who could be supporting them on the farm, were either attending school or had gone off to the townships to work for the white man. As a consequence, the amount of farming still done in my village was reduced to a bare minimum. The general yam barn of the village was abandoned, and only the smaller ones on the individual compounds were retained.

Of all the people in the village, I counted a few men who lived to be really very old. These old men played a crucial role in preserving the ancestral traditions of the village, given that an increasing number of the population were converting to Christianity.

It was a bizarre situation for many children of my age, even though I detected no open conflicts between those who favoured the Christian religion and those who retained the ancestral traditional belief. Adherents to the two religions tolerated each other and existed peacefully side-by-side. For example, the tradition of primogeniture forced my father to abandon Christianity and return to the ancestral traditions; however, everyone else in his family remained Christian. This kind of relationship was characteristic of almost every family in the village.

As Christians, we went to the church of our village every Sunday and participated in all Christian activities. We regularly joined non-Christians to celebrate all festivities in our village, avoiding those areas that might trigger off possible conflicts or contradictions with our Christian religion.

At the traditional level, I watched with interest as the old men serviced the ancestral gods as priests, and maintained law and order in the village as members of the council of elders. Some acquired their positions as priests through heredity, and others were chosen by particular deities for their services.

I was intrigued by the enthusiasm with which these priests-the diviners or traditional healers-executed their duties. They were said to have been empowered with authority, truth, and justice to interpret the wishes of the spirits who blessed and favoured loyal and pious citizens. These spirits punished the offenders of the law and order, as well as those who unwisely transgressed their privileges, and conciliated them with ostentatious offerings.

I noted that, in contrast to our Christian beliefs, the living, the unborn, and the dead were the integral parts of the ancestral religion of the people in my village. They believed that our ancestors lived in a world of the dead that mirrored the world of the living. They offered them sacrifices on various occasions for mediating between them and the gods.

The people assumed that our dead relatives reincarnated into the families of which they had been members whilst they were alive. When a child was born, the parents—usually the father—went to a diviner to help identify whom the child had reincarnated from.

However, as Christians and non-Christians, we celebrated together the cultural festivals on the market day of our village. Our village belonged to the group of villages whose market day was the Nkwo on the traditional Igbo calendar, which has four days, seven weeks, and thirteen months.

The four days of the week are Eke, Orie, Afo, Nkwo, with another four subordinated days. For example, the market day of my father's village was Nkwoba, a subordinate of the Nkwo market day on the traditional Igbo calendar. The market day of my great uncle's village was Orie Amaenyi, a subordinate of the Orie on the traditional Igbo calendar.

Of all the cultural festivities of our village, I most enjoyed the new yam festival, the end of the year festival, and the celebration of our market day, which occurred on a Sunday once in every two months. Whether I was at my great uncle's or in my father's house, we made adequate and rigorous preparations for the events. In the morning of the day of the actual festivity, mothers and their children would occupy themselves intensely in the kitchens beating and grinding various spices with pestles and mortars in preparation for different kinds of special meals. Persistent pounding sounds from the kitchens of the various households filled the air in the village like the music of a folks dance.

Mothers prepared assorted kinds of delicious sauces, vegetable soups, African oil bean salad, and cooked plenty of rice, yams, cocoyams, and cassavas. I helped my stepmother or my great uncle's wife to pound the yams, cocoyams, and the cassavas, which we ate together with the vegetable soups.

We had food in abundance in the house for ourselves and for many of our expected guests. By early afternoon, many relatives and friends from other villages, whose market days were not the same as ours, would begin streaming into our village as guests. They brought with them as presents yams, cocoyams, plantains, and pots and jars of palm wine. In return, we entertained them with food and drink in our individual houses, and with folk songs and dances in the village square.

On their departure, we would prepare and present them with various foods, which we packaged in banana and cocoyam leaves, especially the African oil bean salad with fish and meat, which they took home to share with other relatives who had not been able to accompany them to the festivities.

On this day, all the inhabitants of the village, especially the children, wore their Sunday best and new clothes. As children, we went from house to house, dancing and singing our desire that the food should fill our stomachs instead of remaining in the cooking pots. The people would generously give us food and tips of small amounts of money. We would eat so much food, especially the African oil bean salad, that we would often be sick in the stomach on the following day at school.

The music in the village square would continue long after the guests were gone. The musicians would stroll from house to house, entertaining the inhabitants with music well into the small hours of the morning, and even till dawn. The people would give them generous tips of money; drinks like palm wine, or hot and soft drinks; cola nuts; and African oil bean salad with fish and meat.

Of all the cultural festivals of my village, I took particular great delight in our *ikoro* dance, which was performed on the day of Eke immediately following our end-of-the year festivity. The ikoro was the giant wooden gong of our village. This sacred gong was hollowed out from the log of an iroko tree. It was about four metres long and two metres round and had a long history of exceptional utility to the community as a communication tool during times of war as well as during times of festivity.

Like the iroko tree from which it was made, our ikoro was sacred and highly revered by the community. In 1958, the council of elders of the village considered our present ikoro to be too old to continue in service, and decided that it must be replaced. The young men of a particular age group in our village voluntarily financed the replacement project. They facilitated the purchase of a new ikoro, and built a modern blockhouse with zincked roof for housing it in the village square.

Our new ikoro was bought from a very distant village, where it had been cut, hollowed, chiselled, and polished from the log of a mighty iroko tree. The men of our village spent several days on the road, dragging our new ikoro from its birthplace through many villages and over many hills and streams to our village. They used ropes made from climbing trees, leaves, and branches of palm trees.

On the day the men arrived in our village with the new ikoro, they were greeted with gun salutes, gongs from our aged ikoro, dancing, and singing of war songs by the people.

Replacing an aged ikoro with a young one was not a simple affair. It must happen in strict adherence to the traditions and customs of the people. First, our aged ikoro was interred at the foot of the iroko tree in the village square, and then the young one was ushered into the newly-built, modern blockhouse.

After all the rituals were completed according to the traditions and customs of the people, 30 December 1958 was set for the official funeral of our aged Ikoro, and the inauguration of the young one. It was a big event, to which all the people across the entire Ohuhu community and beyond were invited.

As on all similar occasions, our whole village was meticulously tidied. The little plants and grasses on all the roads of the village were cut and weeded. The women swept and weeded the compounds, painted the walls of their houses with colours made from red and white clay, and drew decorative figures on them with charcoal colours.

Our village square was festooned with flags and colourful cloths hanging from the umbrella trees, the iroko, and the two silk cotton trees with their broad, flat crown of horizontal branches.

As it was in the month of December, the deciduous silk cotton trees were producing beautiful flowers and cottons, which filled the entire village square. The trees had numerous, five-part, pink-and-white flowers that grew in dense clusters and bloomed before the leaves appeared. As children, we enjoyed eating the fruits that later developed, throwing away the seeds and the cotton fibres.

The two silk cotton trees in our village square were over sixty metres high, and had a diameter of about three metres above their buttresses, which can best be described as above-ground roots. The buttresses themselves were about four metres high and extended four metres from the main trunk. They impressively covered a large area on the ground. These natural decorations added to the human efforts that gave our little village the desired festive appearance for the occasion.

As the guests streamed into the village square, they were entertained with drink and food, which were available in abundance. Some of the people drank the wine from the majestic giant pot with gourds, and others, especially the elderly men, with horns of cows. The giant pot was decorated all around with reliefs of different artistic designs. It was said to have existed as far back as the founding days of our village, and was brought out in the public to be seated in the village square only on very special occasions. The giant pot held over a hundred litres of liquid wine at a time, and was kept constantly filled. It was a covenant of truth and unity, peace, fraternity, and goodwill of my village with all people.

The guests brought with them as gifts to my village pots and jars of palm wine, bottles of hot drinks, yams, cash, goats, and fowl. I was the only child of the village that was chosen to work as clerk of the event. My duties were to make a record of the names of the guests and their gifts to our village, and to produce a financial and attendance report at the end of the event.

An adult man, who was one of the members of the group that sponsored the festivity, guided me in my duties.. With hundreds of people watching me as I sat at the table of the clerk of the event, I observed my father's pride in me. I was only thirteen years old. Many of the guests wanted to know whose little boy was seated at the table of the clerk of the festivity. They were surprised when they learned about me, and that I had gone to school from my great uncle's village. I watched from my duty desk as they talked, shook my father's hand, and congratulated him.

As the guests amused themselves, they watched the people of my village perform our traditional war dances and songs, which were intermittently interrupted by the gongs from our young ikoro played by its attendant, an elderly man. At the height of the ceremonies, numerous deafening gun salutes bid farewell to our aged ikoro and welcomed the young one into our village to serve the community for many generations.

After the ikoro festival was held in our village in 1958, my father was even more determined to send me to college after my primary school education. However, he was seriously concerned about his abilities to embark on a college project for me, given his meagre source of income as an ordinary peasant farmer. He could not save enough from his earnings from agricultural produce alone to meet the high financial costs of a secondary school education. Therefore, in addition to farming, he sought other sources of income to increase his earnings. He decided to tap wine from the raffia palm trees on the banks of the main Ikwu River of our village. It was an intensive activity, which required my father to spend many hours of the day on the riverbank vegetation. Once he identified a raffia to be mature for tapping, he constructed a long ladder to reach to its top. Some of the palm trees could grow as high as fifteen metres and higher. When my father reached to the top of the palm tree, he constructed a platform for collecting the wine, or sap. The platform consisted of a mechanism for holding the suspended earthen pot, a belt woven from raffia fibres tied to the branches for him to balance on the top of the tree, and a long rope tied to a branch for transporting the earthen pot up and down.

He would extract the wine by cutting the flower off the raffia palm tree, and fastening the suspended earthen pot to the flower stump, both of which he tightly covered to keep off the bees and other creatures who would be happy to suck away the wine. At weekends and on school holidays, I would leave my great uncle's wife to help my father in collecting the wine. I would spare him the trouble of climbing up and down the ladder several times to transfer the wine from one pot to another. We collected the wine in the evening and in the morning. When we arrived home in the morning from the riverbank, many customers would be waiting impatiently on our compound to buy our wine. Some of them would have placed their orders with my father several days previously.

My father then would mix the morning and evening collections with the appropriate quantity of water to produce several pots and jars of wine, which he would sell to the customers at lucrative prices, always paid to my father with cash money.

As I watched my father go about his daily business, I noticed some heightened nervousness in him. He was otherwise a serene and an introverted person. But, recently, he had become restless and easily irritated. I saw the frustrations and disappointments in his countenance.

I was in my final year at the primary school, and had taken and passed many entrance examinations into various colleges in the country. Regrettably, none of the hosting colleges had offered me a single scholarship. My father could not finance my college education on his own, given his meagre earnings from selling agricultural products and palm wine.

Therefore, my college education posed a big problem for my father, and, at the time, he did not have a practicable solution. As we celebrated Christmas and the end-of-the-year festivity in the village in 1960, I closely observed my father cheering up, as if he had received some revelations of a brighter future. He was not in despair anymore, but seemed to have handed over the fate of his young son to providence for the year ahead.

By token of the same providence in which my father trusted, I came nine years later to Austria, found the opportunities that had hitherto eluded me, grabbed them, and triumphed. As an expression of gratitude to my new country, I resolved to settle, to die, and to be buried in Eichgraben, to remind my reader that I lived in four worlds: my world of childhood and my world of open opportunities, my sighted world and my non-sighted world, whose challenges I squarely mastered with distinction.

www.ingramcontent.com/pod-product-compliance
Lightning Source LLC
Chambersburg PA
CBHW030257290526
45785CB00001B/122